New Directions/ New Dimensions

Florida Writers Association Collection, Volume 17

New Directions/ New Dimensions

Florida Writers Association Collection, Volume 17

Florida Writers Association

Winter Park, Florida

Foreword

2025—what a year, and what a collection of writing from our membership who endured a deluge of winds, rains, floods, tornadoes, and hurricanes in 2024. Perhaps it's that devastation which brought us some of the most heartfelt writing that I've read in my three years as executive editor of this book.

This, the 17th edition of our members' best creative nonfiction (CNF), fiction, and poetry, lives up to the mantra stated by our founders twenty-four years ago: With *writers helping writers* the best that writers have to offer will emerge. And the *best* is evident in this collection.

I cannot fully express my gratitude to our adult and NextGen members for sharing their personal possessions: their words, their emotions, their most inner thoughts. In this book you'll find stories that bare the soul of the author.

The CNF submissions may be the most revealing. Some of the pieces take the theme literally, with a story like "New Roads" where a boy on a bicycle finds a new friend outside his staid middle-class neighborhood. Then there's a piece about a man who overcomes his fear of risk-taking while dancing with a cross-dresser at a 1970s dive bar: a life changing event.

This year's fiction submissions range from the sublime, as in "The Midnight Gardener" where flowers unexpectantly bloom and butterflies flutter, to the scary where a book in "Stop Reading—Now!" may prove fatal.

The CNF and fiction entries were outstanding, but that empress of language . . . that epitome of words: poetry is equally impressive. Reading the section of verse collected herein, I've come to appreciate how our contributors are able to mold language to let the reader experience the world with new senses. "Upon the Loss of an Old Friend" incorporates jazz rhythms; "Maroon Moccasins" is full of color, full of vibrant life; "Fledgling" uniquely weaves verses to tell the story of a mother-daughter relationship.

I hope you enjoy *New Directions/New Dimensions* as much as I did while I edited it. And I invite you to join us with a submission in 2026 to Collection 18, *Fragments*.

Paul Iasevoli, Collection 17 Executive Editor

Content Advisory

Some material in this publication deals with situations and topics which may not be considered suitable for children or sensitive individuals, discretion is advised

Table of Contents

POETRY

NEXTGEN POETRY

CONTRIBUTOR BIOS

CREATIVE NONFICTION

Should Old People Plant Blueberries?

by Gerri Almand

I'm an old woman from the Deep South who recently settled in the Pacific Northwest, and I wanted to grow blueberries. The Oregon State University Extension Service website promised that blueberries would thrive in this climate and produce "pounds of delicious fruit all season long." I'd already heard neighbors bragging about their prodigious annual blueberry bounties. My heart raced and my breath quickened.

In the garden section of Jerry's Home Improvement Center last spring, I happened upon lush, blossom-laden blueberry bushes. My pulse accelerated as I considered the potential. A mere three plants, and I could be giving away blueberries by August and still have plenty to stuff into my own bottomless tummy.

I drooled at the thought of walking into my backyard and picking berries off the bush. Standing in that aisle at Jerry's, it took all the self-discipline I could muster not to grab as many bushes as would fit into my car. I opted, however, to learn more about blueberry cultivation before digging my Visa card from my purse and holes in my backyard.

Within the first five minutes of my online research, dreams of delicious blueberries by next summer dissolved. The Extension Service said I should prune those lovely, flower-laden bushes from Jerry's down to four or five canes and remove every single bud. The explanation made sense. During its first year, the plant needed to spend its energy growing roots and shoots, not producing fruit.

The Extension Service further reported that it could take a couple of years for a bush to produce any fruit at all and that it took at least seven years for a bush to reach maturity. Given that the lifespan of a blueberry bush was about fifty years, I understood why it would behoove a gardener to delay the immediate gratification of first-season production in favor of higher long-term yields in every possible scenario . . . except one.

What if the planter of blueberry bushes was old and not sure she'd live another seven years? Someone . . . well, like me.

If I planted blueberries in my backyard, I wanted to grab huge delicious berries from my plants the next summer, not several years down the road. I wanted to savor the taste, the smell, the sound of the pop as my teeth burst each berry's skin, and the feel of its juice dripping down my chin. When it came to blueberries, I had no patience for delayed gratification. I was already seventy-four years old, and I didn't have time to waste.

It stunned me to realize I might be too old to plant blueberries. My mind flashed to myriad other dreams that'd never materialize in the short time I had left to live—living abroad, earning a PhD, serving in the Peace Corps, and creating a yard in Oregon that I'd love half as much as I had loved the one in Florida. My angst had nothing to do with blueberries. It was about my mortality.

Sometimes, when the weather is nice and my ninety-four-year-old neighbor Winifred is sitting in the sunshine in her driveway, I walk across the street and visit. During my last driveway chat, I shared my dilemma about wanting to plant blueberries but not being sure I had enough years left.

"Let me tell you a story," Winifred said. "When my mother was about your age, she decided she didn't like the afternoon sun shining in her bedroom, so she planted a tree outside her window." Winifred paused and looked me in the eye. "Everybody laughed at my mother, saying she'd never live long enough for that tree to provide shade. But my mother was right. She lived another twenty years, and when she passed away, it was in the afternoon, lying on her bed and looking out her window at that thirty-foot tree that now shaded her window."

It took me a minute to respond. "That's an inspiring story," I finally said. "It reminds me of that old saying about planting a tree being a belief in the future. Maybe I should plant blueberries with the idea of making the next owners of my house happy, huh?"

Winifred smiled.

"Or maybe plant them believing that I'll be picking and eating my own blueberries for many years."

"There you go," my wise friend said.

With a new resolve, I left Winifred's driveway determined to follow my blueberry dreams. I believed I could prune a blossom-heavy bush down to the nub and focus on long-term rather than immediate rewards. For the next couple of years, I'd just make trips to nearby blueberry farms or to my neighborhood WinCo to satisfy my blueberry cravings.

I again tackled the Extension Service website and realized anew that I was far from ready to bring home even one of those robust blueberry bushes from Jerry's.

Location, soil, and pH were the most important cultural factors. I studied my backyard, tracing the sun's path, trying to anticipate its trajectory as the seasons changed. My blueberries would need at least six full hours of sun daily, preferably more. In time, I decided my southern fencerow would work.

The next hurdle proved more vexing. It seems that blueberries are particular about soil, especially little things like drainage and acidity. For drainage, the plants like to stay damp but would not tolerate sitting in water. As I walked along my selected blueberry site, my shoes squished in the rain-saturated soil. I doubted those blueberries would like their feet staying wet any more than I would.

Finally, I learned that blueberries liked acidic soil and that I should begin testing my soil at least a year before I planned to plant. The lab results would give readings on the important nutrients and how much of what to add to the soil to make my blueberries happy. This soil testing, amending, re-testing, and re-amending could take a couple of years before all the readings fell within the recommended parameters. By now, the very thought of planting blueberries was making me weary.

The bottom line, end-of-the-discussion, final deal-breaker on planting blueberries came when I revisited the math and took note of my age, which by now was seventy-five. If I rushed out and snatched up several blueberry bushes and planted them this afternoon, taking my chances on drainage, pH, and soil quality, and if I did the recommended initial severe pruning, I'd probably be seventy-seven or seventy-eight before I plucked the first delicious, sun-warmed blueberry from a bush in my backyard. Even more depressing, I'd be eighty-two before my bushes reached maturity and gave me their best.

A few weeks later, I noticed in my daily email queue a new online seminar offered by the Extension Service titled "Picky Fruit: Establishing Blueberries in a Home Garden." Given my current disappointment over all I'd recently learned about the possibility of a lovely blueberry patch in my backyard, I sighed at the irony. I could only laugh that even the Extension Service was now using the term "picky" to describe those damnable bushes. What had happened to that earlier promise that this area was a blueberry grower's paradise?

But did it really matter if I'd be eighty-two when the results of my labors reached full fruition? Winifred's mother had believed in the future, and that faith rewarded her with lovely afternoon shade for her bedroom window because she'd planted a tree while in her mid-seventies.

I vowed to plant some blueberry bushes.

But alas, the weather turned warmer, and I missed the best window for planting blueberries that spring. But my desire to plant something edible in my yard proved unrelenting, so I headed back to Jerry's, found a fig tree on sale, and plopped it down in the area I'd earmarked for blueberries. I'd learned from the Extension Service website that figs weren't finicky about soil and would produce well by their second year. I wanted to believe that I'd enjoy gorging myself with figs as much as I would have loved devouring fistfuls of blueberries.

I haven't told Winifred about my blueberry change of heart. I'm too embarrassed. I can only hope that if I live to ninety-six, I will have grown as wise as my friend and will feel young enough to plant blueberries. It could happen.

Past Life

by Deborah Crutcher

Standing in the middle of a dingy, dark theater alone, I asked myself, "How did I get here?" A blinding light appeared in the center of the movie screen framed by burgundy velvet curtains. Looking down at my feet, I was shocked to see big, brown men's shoes. Shoes I called clodhoppers. I was wearing a long, raggedy trench coat. *What the . . . I am a man.*

The theater went dark immediately. Frightened, I searched for the door and ran. Once outside, I floated above the ground in total darkness.

That was not a dream. It was how my first past-life regression session began. People told me I was "an old soul," someone who seemed wiser than their years. It indicates that your soul has been on this Earth before. Some people with old souls feel as if they don't fit in. At other times, a new environment may seem eerily familiar. There have been times when I instantly connected with someone I had never met, which sparked the idea that perhaps this person and I had traveled together in past lives.

Have you ever been to a new place and felt you'd been there before? Some call these synchronicities. It's the concept that our soul lives on in multiple lifetimes. Many believe that traumas, memories, and feelings pass from one life to another. Past life regression therapy can help release those blocked emotions—the demons you pushed down and locked up.

Always curious about past lives and their impact on us today, I read that when we experience déjà vu, it's our spirit guides or ancestors giving us signs that we are on the right path. Our guides help us if we open our hearts and minds and listen.

Alana, an employee of Moon Dreamz, a metaphysical store, was my guide for this session. She recently relocated from Hawaii to Florida. Her beautiful Polynesian skin and light-brown hair with golden highlights lit up her glowing smile, emitting a joyful radiance.

Alana placed me in a state of light hypnosis while I lay on a comfortable, warm bed. Her soft, firm voice relaxed me as she instructed me to stare at an overhead light. Though in a light trance, I was still aware of my surroundings and could speak.

After the movie theater experience, my spiritual leader counted one, two, three and snapped her fingers. Now, there were waves. I was alone in a small cabin cruiser-sized boat in the middle of a dark sea. The derelict boat was stripped of lights and instruments and had no motor. I looked over the gunnel, and one bright light shone from a deep hole in the ocean floor. At first, I was scared but then curious as if I could see all the way through to the other side of the planet.

The light slowly faded to a dot, then disappeared, leaving me in darkness. I slid to the floor, wrapped in blackness and silence. "I'm dying!" I cried. "I am dying now." My sobbing was uncontrollable.

Alana told me to take deep breaths and relaxed me back into my trance with "one, two, three." *Snap.*

I instantly changed from hysterically crying to laughing and smiling. "Where are you now?" Alana asked. "What's so funny?'

"I'm flying. It's blissful. Dense green trees line both sides of a winding stream. There's no civilization in this rich forest. Flying is so freeing. Wait, wait, I'm coming down."

Imagine the scenery from the movies *Avatar* and *Maleficent* blended. That's where I landed—lush grass among towering, robust trees with wide branches reaching out to touch their neighbors. The air was fresh with the lingering scents of honeysuckle that grew along the banks of the nearby rippling water. Colorful butterflies and birds fluttered in the sun's golden rays, with fairies darting in and out of the foliage.

"This is so peaceful and beautiful; I've been here before," I said, awestruck.

"Now that you have landed, look down at your feet; what do you see?" Alana said.

"Uh . . . well, they aren't feet. They're big, strong talons. "Oh, my goodness, I'm an eagle," I said, flapping my long wings.

The smell of a campfire pulled me deeper into a canopy of trees. Time slowed. The farther I entered this world, the more magical and mysterious it became. The soft forest floor cushioned my steps as I approached a plush little grove with images sitting in a circle on a log. I was grateful to see my spirit animals, a friendly red fox, and a gray wolf with a black nose, warming themselves around the fire. These animals had been with me on previous shamanic meditative journeys.

In the distance, a woman wearing a long, flowing white gown appeared. Her shiny black hair fell to her waist as she glided inches above the forest floor, moving in and out of the trees as if she were hiding, never showing her face. The mystery woman's image dimmed, then disappeared. "Was that me?" I asked Alana.

Black clouds fell over the forest, bringing waves of darkness. I tried to see the sun and asked, "Is my whole world filled with darkness?" Floating in a dark hole, I was dying again.

"One, two, three." *Snap.*

Daylight.

Once I was calm, Alana said, "You are in a long hallway with many doors. Make them any color or style you want. Walk down that hallway, open the door, and tell me what you see."

I walked toward a bright-red door with a brass lion's head knocker and opened the door with trepidation. *What was I getting into now?*

Upon entering, I felt as though I was in someone's home, a place I had never been before. The furniture was heavy dark wood, with many curios on lacy-topped tables and a filled bookcase. It was a big, two-story country house. An old, frail, gray-haired woman sat on a vintage sofa, peering into space. She looked so sad.

"Who is she?" asked Alana.

"I don't know. She's not my grandmother." I sat beside the older lady and took her hand; she was silent and never looked at me.

"How old are you?" Alana said.

"I am a young woman, around thirty years old." I looked at the despondent lady next to me. "Is this a future me?" I asked, tears welling up in my eyes.

"One, two, three." *Snap*.

I'm floating again, no longer an eagle. I'm flying among a vast group of lightning bugs flashing green as they call out for a mate. I was having fun darting and dashing among these flying creatures.

Flying horizontally, barely off the ground, I gained speed. Suddenly, I turned upward and zoomed toward a sky crowded with stars. My body was compressed as if I were in a tight capsule. Since there was no moon, the stars were brilliant. Then I stopped moving and just floated in space among the stardust.

"One, two, three." *Snap*.

That was the end of the two-hour session as Alana gradually brought me back to the present moment. She asked me what I thought my themes were in this session.

After pondering this question, I realized I was faced with much darkness. I considered myself fearless, especially given all my adventurous activities, such as jumping off high cliffs into dark water, scuba diving among sharks, or diving 138 feet down the Blue Hole in Belize.

Rock climbing, snow skiing in the Alps, or running the slalom course in a water ski competition are all things I did with excitement. Obtaining a French visa at the age of sixty and moving to the South of France for a year was a challenging experience that I faced with enthusiasm, not fear.

Ironically, besides snakes, my biggest fear is dying alone. Alana explained that I am never alone and have never been. My spirit guides have been with me since the day I was born.

I am a spiritual person and strive to live a spiritual lifestyle. I meditate daily and seek to demonstrate kindness, compassion, forgiveness, and love—including self-love—through my actions. After this session, I became more aware of myself, and my meditations took a new direction. There is a feeling of fullness where emptiness once was. Self-love is my priority. When helping others, I remember not to forget my own needs.

Now Streaming

by Margaret Daisley

SCENE: A Midwestern university town in the 1950s. It's not unusual to see people who don't look like me—white—in the stores where I shop, in the church and school I attend, and especially on campus, where there is a large population of international students and my dad is a professor.

MUSIC: Radio: "Rock of Ages;" local and farm news; Doris Day, "Que Sera, Sera."

My first year in school, some of us huddle together on the playground. One girl has a Hershey's candy bar she generously offers to share. I suggest the shy girl standing next to me, Judy, would love some. Judy's skin is brown, and in my naïve way of thinking, unexposed so far to the idea of hate—except when a sibling gets a bigger piece of cake—I had concluded Judy must love Hershey's, because her skin is the color of milk chocolate.

The grade school we attend offers free music lessons in piano and stringed instruments—violin, viola, cello, bass. My mother, always one to take advantage of opportunities to partake of "culture," requires us to take piano, but—magnanimously—allows us our choice of stringed instrument. She also enrolls us in Saturday Musicales, part of a statewide program in which young musicians meet at someone's home once a month to perform for their peers from various schools.

MUSIC: "Für Elise," Clementi sonatinas.

Prepubescent girls dress for Saturday Musicales as if going to Sunday school. The boys get cleaned up, too, but a few are rowdy cutups, with shirttails hanging out and mussed hair. In particular the twins, Bob and Tad, who variously sample piano, singing, and marimba, seem more interested in getting laughs than in developing musical talents or fine-tuning their social skills.

I make friends—an acquaintance—with another girl, Nyla. She goes to a different school, and is a Negro, a term I had learned by then. I find I have much more in common with Nyla than with the clowns (though we both laugh at them) or even most of the other non-Negro girls who are from the other side of town and wear better, newer dresses.

In junior high, Judy—who "loves chocolate"—and I become mentor-helpers for a Brownie troop, and after the meetings we walk to the bus together. Our families go to the same Catholic church and school. Her older brother is an altar boy with my older brother. Her younger sister is in my younger sister's class.

These are some of the people who populate my life's story. They're not my best friends. They're just part of my community. We swim in the same pond.

MUSIC: Chubby Checker, "The Twist;" The Beatles, "Twist and Shout;" Peter, Paul & Mary, "If I Had a Hammer."

We watch TV and read *Life* and *Time* and our daily newspaper as the Civil Rights battles are fought on the streets of Birmingham, Selma, and Little Rock. I've never set foot in any of the Southern states. They are as foreign to me as Gaza and Ukraine are foreign to me now. I am barely a teenager. I wonder what is wrong with "those Southerners" that they can treat people this way.

In high school, there are many more types of kids, not just non-Catholics, and not just nice girls, but a wide array—athletic, rebellious, studious, creative, comic, entrepreneurial. Many African American boys are on the sports teams. There is at least one teacher who is African American. In my junior year, a beautiful African American girl, Donna, is elected Basketball Queen. I feel a sense of pride. In my hometown, I think, we don't have that terrifying racism they have "down South."

MUSIC: Simon & Garfunkel, "Sounds of Silence."

On a date after I graduate from high school, the young man I've been fixed up with has his pilot's license, and we go for an hour's flight in a tiny two-seater. It seems so exciting at first, but when he says, leeringly, the plan is to buzz the local nudist colony, he begins to lose my respect. And then, as we are calling it a day, he tells me a story about a recent date. When he'd taken the girl home, he tells me, he saw "niggers" sitting on the front porch. "What are those niggers doing there?" he'd asked his date. "Those are my parents," she'd explained. And as he tells this story, his lip curls in disgust. He looks at me as if expecting a kindred spirit, but I feel only shock. I don't know how to respond. I am repelled. I can't get away fast enough.

MUSIC: Ray Charles, "Hit the Road, Jack;" Lovin' Spoonful, "Hot Town, Summer in the City."

In my sophomore year of college at the university in my hometown, I'm reading the local newspaper. When I come to the back page, I suddenly feel I have been transported to another place, another time—jerked out of the present and thrown into a foreign, unfamiliar world. There, taking up the whole back page of the newspaper, is a paid advertisement by the local Ku Klux Klan, with photos of key members, hoods raised, faces exposed. It is an announcement of their plans to have a rally on the courthouse lawn.

KKK members in my town? What is this—the South? Isn't all "that" behind us?

I am gobsmacked. Afraid.

MUSIC: Ben E. King, "Stand by Me;" James Brown, "Say It Loud."

I'm working at the library on campus along with my old friend from Saturday Musicales, Nyla. We discuss the KKK threat and agree we have no choice. We must go to the rally together, if only to stand in protest. But we're scared.

At the same time, I'm dating one of the university's football players. He calls and asks if I can borrow my parents' car to give somebody a ride. When I show up at his dorm, it turns out it's the Black football players who need a ride to the local Baptist church where there's going to be a meeting to discuss the KKK threat. No whites are invited. Just the mayor.

Sanity prevails. The mayor refuses to grant the KKK a permit to gather. The threat and hysteria gradually die down, but then I learn that people, Black and white, have been talking about "arming themselves." It is much worse than I had imagined.

MUSIC: Marvin Gaye, "What's Going On."

At a high school reunion, I ask Nyla if she remembers this incident with the KKK. Of course she does. We'd been expecting it, she tells me—she and her relatives, her friends, and other people of color in the community. This was part of their lives. It had been simmering there all along, but I had only seen rare glimpses of it when it broke the surface, like a fish jumping out of the water to catch a bug.

MUSIC: Sam Cooke, "A Change is Gonna Come."

I now live in a city on the Gulf Coast of Florida. I take a tour of the historical Black area and learn that schools and pools weren't integrated, and Blacks were restricted to living within a proscribed area until the Civil Rights Act passed in 1965—the year Donna became Basketball Queen at my high school. The tour also highlights a historical plaque which lets us know that right here on this spot a Black man was lynched in 1914, accused of murdering a white person, but never arrested or tried. Just lynched and then shot, too, because he didn't die right away.

When I was young, I would have reacted to these facts like a typical white Yankee who had never been exposed to the realities of Jim Crow. I would have said something like, *I thought the Civil War ended in 1865!* But now I know it took another 100 years for the Civil Rights Act to pass, and even that didn't suddenly reverse the course of the incoming surge.

It also took about half that many years for me to realize that history isn't just something that happened in the past, to other people, in far-away places. It's this pool we're all in together, swimming with or against the currents, and sometimes going out with the tide.

MUSIC: Anna Nalin, chorus only, "Breath (2 AM)" and fade.

Fridays with Jack

by David Godin

My Friday calendar entry simply states, "Golf-Jack." Our tee time is usually around 11 a.m. because Jack doesn't get up early. We play only the par-three, nine-hole courses in The Villages because they are short and have no greens fees; however, even these present a challenge for our limited skills.

Besides Jack, a spry eighty-three, and me, the kid of our foursome at sixty-eight, our group is rounded out by Lee, who recently turned eighty-three himself, and Glenn, Jack's brother-in-law. I estimate Glenn to be in his late seventies. Jack sets up the tee times and selects the course to play, which is fine by me. I am well past the desire to be in charge and am content to follow.

Each of us has a distinct style. Jack, tall and thin, most resembles a five-foot-ten-inch heron. He is a retired postal letter carrier who walked thousands of miles during his career, but he opts to ride in a golf cart these days. Jack's swing is a wide arc, and he can hit a long ball. Sometimes the ball flies straight, and sometimes it arcs sideways, veering left and coming back. It's the coming back we find so fascinating. Will it? Won't it? We never know. We watch Jack's ball in flight as if he had thrown a last-minute Hail Mary pass to a well-covered receiver, and we all have money on the game. Jack's ball rarely finds the green.

I play global military golf. It's global golf when I tee off because I strike the globe several inches behind the tee before hitting the ball. According to the self-appointed and vocal swing coaches I golf with, I lean back and hit the ball like Sammy Sosa, aiming for the back fence. As I march from tee to green, the ball flies left, right, left, right in true military fashion. I avoid the fairway where the ball might be exposed to my foe, the hole, and instead place it in the landscaping or sand trap, where it has cover and concealment, allowing me to assault the green while maintaining the element of surprise.

Glenn, whose real name is Howard, isn't as flexible as he used to be, like the rest of us, I suppose. I don't know why he doesn't go by his first name, but Jack's wife Gae doesn't use hers either. Her real first name is Laura. I've asked both him and Gae if they are in witness protection, but I've received only denials. Glenn plays a great short game. His tee shot is short of the fairway, his chip shots are short of the green, and his putts are short of the cup. Glenn's backswing makes up in speed what it lacks in accuracy. His aim is consistently inconsistent, which means the ball travels at the mercy of which part of the club face he hits it with.

Lee is lean like Jack, but taller. He punches rather than swings at the ball. Both legs collapse as he swings, like a crane fishing along the shore. His shots accelerate from the club low to the ground. Worms and small insects on the course fear his ball. On the green he follows a similar technique, which I call punch and go. He punches at the ball with his putter and then goes after it like he's gonna race it to the hole. His punches rarely result in the ball falling in the cup, and he'll make a couple of attempts before giving up.

Lee, whose main goal is just to get out, is casual about keeping score. He's been a bit lonely since his wife died about six months ago, but he looks better. His wife had dementia, and caring for her was a heavy burden for him.

In short, we are a pathetic crew, and nobody expects to get a PGA tour card. Nobody but Glenn keeps the scorecard or calculates a handicap. But we aren't too worried about it. I have given it some thought, over a post-round beer or two, and I figure golf is like sex—everybody wants to play, very few are any good at it, and a small number of people get paid to do it. As for my group, we know we aren't getting paid, and we know we aren't any good. But we want to play. We live for that one good shot, the moment of bliss, the sweet thwack of the club on the ball, the ball traveling, impossibly straight, exactly in the right direction, at the right speed, and the right distance, and you know it's a good shot from the moment the club face contacts the ball. We tell ourselves it's intentional and not a happy accident. That one good shot is all we need to bring us back next week, and most of the golfers we know agree.

I know our weekly golf game won't go on forever. We are all older and more fragile and just one fall in the kitchen or a slip on the sidewalk away from the end of our golf career. I am already mourning that day.

New Roads

by John Hope

"**G**et out," Mom snapped at me. Vacuum in one hand, a dust rag in the other, and sweat dripping down the sides of her head; her reddened face showed no room for debating. The first Saturday of the month always meant house cleaning day, and Mom had no patience for a ten-year-old boy messing up her work.

I dashed out to the garage, mounted my bike, and was off, ready to explore roads and neighborhoods alien to me—the farther the better.

The first few streets were the same ol' same ol'. I passed my friend Alice's house, sped past the goofy Nelson twins' place, rounded the DMV, and trekked around the water treatment plant.

I hopped off my bike to cross the busy 66th Street. Remounting my seat, I took a fresh breath and ventured down unknown roads.

My mind flurried with memories of past biking adventures. Like the time I came upon a big group of kids playing tag in front of a house cluttered with parked cars. I hopped off my bike and joined in, dashing through the yard and taking turns being *it*. After a few minutes, a lady at the front door called for the kids to come inside. A couple kids jostled me toward the door. I stepped into the middle of a crowded living room. A man stood in the hallway pointing a camera at the crowd and said, "Ready? Say cheese." We all smiled, and he snapped a few pictures. After I left, I realized what had just happened and wondered if anyone would ever notice the random kid in what was probably a family portrait.

And then there was the time I befriended a different group of kids and convinced them I was a recent immigrant from Siberia. I called myself Ivan and spoke with a Russian accent. The kids were thrilled. They held up balls and jump ropes and asked me to translate the names of things into Russian. I'd make up some gobbledygook and they repeated my nonsense to their siblings. Fortunately, I high-tailed it home before they caught on.

But now, after traveling through yet another unexplored neighborhood of houses, yards, fences, and the occasional yapping dog, I started to worry. The houses grew dilapidated, the yards were weedy, and sidewalks were cracked and gnarled with mold. Everything looked like it could use Mom's scrubbing.

I slowed and considered U-turning it home.

I spotted a boy crouching over a concrete gutter separating the road from the sidewalk. His intense focus on the gutter made me wonder what he was up to. I wheeled up next to him and straddled my bike.

Squinting, he looked up from what looked like a pile of sticks in the gutter.

I asked, "Whatcha doin'?"

He smiled, revealing a gap between his two front teeth. "Making a dam." He pointed up the road. "Here it comes."

A fresh line of water sped down the gutter toward the boy's pile of sticks. A couple houses down, squirting sprinklers fed the stream. The water hit the boy's dam, stopping it cold. The incoming water swelled to a tiny pond that spilled out into the road. But the swelling didn't stop, and it threatened to overtake the dam.

"Quick!" The boy raced up the yard. "More sticks!"

I jumped off my bike and gathered sticks with the boy.

When we returned to the dam, the water had already broken through, pushing the sticks and carrying some of the barrier with it.

"Farther down," I called as I ran down to the gutter that hadn't yet gotten water. I started a new dam with my collection.

The boy joined in, crisscrossing his sticks with mine just as the water struck. It pooled at the new dam, but only for a moment. Water seeped through the cracks.

In desperation, I shoveled dirt from the nearby yard with my hands and packed it against the sticks. This stopped the seepage, but only for a moment before the newly formed mud broke apart, allowing the water to pass.

"Danny!" a woman's voice called from a couple houses down. "Lunch!"

Danny looked saddened by the news.

I said, "I can keep building."

"You want a PB&J sandwich? My mom can make you one."

I rolled my tongue and imagined the fresh taste of peanut butter and sweet jelly. "Sure."

I nodded and followed him back to his house.

After some strenuous begging, Danny's mom caved and welcomed me in. We plopped down onto side-by-side chairs at a small kitchen table. Rather than make a second sandwich, Danny's mom cut his sandwich, and we each munched on our half. She gave us our own cup of red Kool-Aid.

I winced at the chunky peanut butter and weird-tasting jelly that was nothing like the sandwiches my mom made.

"Wha' you mame?" Danny asked with a peanut butter mouth.

"John."

He sipped his Kool-Aid and smiled his lip-stained approval.

Once we gulped down the last of our lunch, Danny said, "Wanna play Legos?"

I nodded.

We shot down the hallway, but Danny stopped at an opened door that didn't look like a kid's bedroom. Inside, opened cardboard boxes cluttered the room, overstuffed with clothes, trophies, books, and other random things.

Danny lost his toothy smile.

"What . . ." I started.

He glided into the room as if pulled in by an invisible force.

I hesitated, then followed.

Danny flipped open the lid to one of the boxes and slipped out a picture frame. I peered over his shoulder to see a younger, laughing Danny, shirtless in a bathing suit. A muscular guy, too young to be a dad, held him up from behind. A sunny beach and foaming waves rounded out the photo.

"Who's that?" I asked.

"My . . . brother . . ." His voice trembled.

Something stirred beneath his words. Like sticks holding back the water, I knew his curled lips wouldn't hold.

He pulled out another framed photo—this one only had Danny's brother dressed in a sharp blue-and-white military uniform, his face stern and focused. Tears dripped on the glass. Danny's damp face pulsed red, ready to burst.

I shifted. Unlike the dam, I couldn't just scoop some dirt.

Danny dropped the frame and attacked me.

I held my breath as he squeezed me in a full-body hug. He shivered and cried into my shoulder. Stunned, my hands floated at first, then slowly curled around him.

"Oh, Danny," his mom said from the hall.

Danny released me and sprang to his mom, wrapping his arms around her.

I remained in the room, feeling exposed with my dampened shoulder.

Danny's mom wiped tears from her face and nodded to me. "You better head home."

That night, I lay in bed. Mom's disinfected house tickled my nose as it always did the first Saturday of the month.

Dad stepped into my room and reached for the light switch. "Good night, John."

"Dad?"

"Yes?"

I searched for the right words to describe what happened at Danny's house. I knew each of my biking adventures always led me down unfamiliar roads, but this one was the weirdest. Something happened that day—a flood of emotions that didn't belong to me. Yet, I was welcomed in and got to see something not as Spic-and-Span as the home I was used to.

"What is it, John?"

"Did . . . did you used to ride your bike when you were ten?"

He smiled and leaned into the doorframe. "I rode down all sorts of streets."

"Really?"

"Oh, yeah. Thing is, if you only stay around the places you know, you'll never learn how other people live. Understand who they are. What they're going through." He paused. "Did you see anything today?"

"A crying boy."

He lowered his brow. "Did you make him cry?"

"No."

"Did you help him?"

"Uh . . . I guess so."

"Good. Then maybe he can be there for you next time *you* cry."

"Yeah."

Dad clicked off the light. "Good night, John." He walked off.

I wasn't sure if I completely understood what Danny was going through and what might have happened to his brother. But as I waited for sleep to come, I yearned to venture even farther on my bike, down different roads with new adventures, and possibly revisit places like Danny's to learn more and understand who he is.

And maybe I wouldn't wait until Mom cleans the house.

Joy in a Time of Sorrow

by Sharon Keller Johnson

A condo at the beach had always been my husband Larry's dream. Then, fourteen years ago, we found one we could afford. We bought it and planned to sell our house and move to Ponce Inlet after Larry retired. I painted the front rooms in soft turquoise and greens, the sea colors that always brought me calm and peace. Larry chose forest colors of browns and dark greens for our bedroom. It was like falling asleep in a tall tree bower. We filled the place with books, paintings, and our most treasured knickknacks. It became our hobbit hole in the sky, our haven. At the time, I was my parents' caregiver, and the condo was a refuge from the stress while still being able to reach Mom and Dad if an emergency arose.

Whenever we had time, we would drive to the beach, watch the birds soar, and listen to the crashing waves. Something about the ocean always comforted my spirit. Larry and I would read books, share ideas, and soak in God's beautiful creation and each other. Our family and friends joined us, and the condo became a center for reunions and family vacations. It was our slice of Heaven on earth.

We never moved out to Ponce. When our daughter Kiki died, we decided to remain in Lake County a little longer to help the husband and sons she left behind.

Then Parkinson's disease crept in, almost without my notice. Larry was an emergency room doctor and a brilliant diagnostician, yet he ignored his own symptoms. Only when the tremors became noticeable to me did he finally admit what it was. At first, the disease seemed to have little impact. We could still walk down to the beach, but it grew more difficult for my husband. Eventually, it became impossible.

Larry refused to entertain the idea of selling the condo. He still hoped he could regain his mobility and return to Ponce Inlet.

Parkinson's disease is different for each person, almost like an imaginative executioner. Larry suffered from tremors, and the man who could fix anything lost his ability to accomplish the most simple task that required fine motor skills. My husband would drive somewhere once and forever remembered the route. Now, he became confused with directions. I watched as his speech slowed and his vocabulary slipped away. He somehow remained coherent until the last couple of months, but an excruciating pain in his hips and back made life unbearable for us both.

Larry never wanted to go into a nursing home, and I agreed with him. Our final parting was rushing toward us faster than I had imagined. I cherished being in the same bed with him, watching television and snuggling. Eventually, it took its toll. Sleep became nothing more than a myth, and I watched as my husband crumbled and floated away.

Larry died on a Friday.

We had been married for forty-six years, had grown up together, discovered the world together, and grew deeper into God together. So much of *me* had become *we*.

My brilliant, handsome, funny, hard-working husband was gone. Half of me ceased to function as if I had suffered some emotional, spiritual stroke. With Larry dead, what was left?

For the first months, I was in a haunted stage. I swear I heard his voice. It felt as if he was right around the corner or back in our bedroom. That eventually dissipated. Only once in a while do I still imagine he's in the next room, or I sense him in bed next to me.

So here it is, almost ten months later. I am a follower of Christ and know this world is only temporary. The next one will have no grief, no death, and no separation. I can't wait until that new age dawns. In the meantime, I sit here, alone. Well, not quite alone.

I've learned grief is only for a season. My sister-in-law calls these "the short years" because they fly by so fast. I will be reunited with my husband sooner than I realize.

God used my grief to draw me closer to Him. As a child, I was preoccupied by suffering. I was born with pernicious anemia and went undiagnosed for ten years. I was acutely aware of suffering, but I also became aware of a God who watched over me. I have found joy in each of my griefs—the joy of God's presence and the wonder of witnessing Him work in my life. I lost my husband, but not my God.

Then again, I haven't even lost Larry. He is still here—in the way I think, cook, and see others. The parts of *me* that became *we* are still *we*. Larry has changed and deepened me as a person, and his death did not take that away. So now, I approach new situations as not simply *me* but as a new *me/we*.

I know that despite all my problems and the people I've lost, there can always be more suffering. But I also know I am safe in the hands of my ever-watchful God, who loves me and brought me into his family through his suffering, death, and resurrection.

This month I sat at the end of the condo's dining room table, staring at a pile of papers as if they were execution orders. As two real estate agents smiled at me from across the table, I signed the papers.

Deciding to sell the condo wasn't easy, but it was necessary. Since Larry's death, the bills have been piling up, and I could no longer keep up both my house and the condo. One had to go. When I signed the paper that cold, rainy January morning, I thought the world was crying with me.

My brother, Tim, had a saying. As Christians, we know, "Our bad things will work out for good. Our good things cannot be taken away, and the best things are yet to come."

Joy and excitement are always mine, even in the midst of grief. And that is something I'll never lose.

Where the Compass Breaks

by Brenda K. Lavieri

The universe is always right. To the perceptive observer it might seem ironic, karmic, or even deserved. But is the so-called "silver lining" always the afterthought rather than the beauty itself? Did Jason's internal compass steer him wrong or did he lose sight of true north, sending his ship aground?

His thoughts swirled as he sang goofily through his final work hours, completely high—literally—on a scaffold, fueled by a Four Loko malt liquor lunch. He believed it was just another day, but it wasn't. As he applied the final brush strokes to the ceiling of St. John's Church on Silver Street, an unseen truth lingered. This task was his crescendo. His last masterpiece was more than pain—it was a prelude. Though he did not know it, he was preparing to share the secret gifts he had held quietly for a lifetime.

The universe has a way of delivering what is needed—even when it arrives as a hard-knock blip on life's radar. That static signal then goes radio silent, no longer traceable, splintering into oblivion like withering fireworks.

Jason and I grew up in central New York. I lived in town, and he lived near our grandparents' Tanner Hill dairy farm where his father and my mother had grown up as siblings. As the elder cousin to many, I babysat

Jason when we were young and spent the entire summer after I graduated with his family. He was shy and kindhearted, and that gentle way about him always stayed with me.

Perhaps it was by cosmic design and through family turmoil that Jason would discover ways to numb his feelings and construct self-reliance for what lay ahead. Immediately after graduating high school, he moved to Florida with his girlfriend and made resilience his armor.

Over the next two decades, I would reach out sporadically, checking in with an open heart and mind. Once I called the Jacksonville Sheriff's Office requesting a welfare check, and a few days later Jason contacted me. "Just seeing if you're alive, cuz," I joked with him as he responded in appreciation. Jason was a pleasant soul, a voracious reader, and a talented carpenter who experienced homelessness. His childhood was woven with hurt and disappointment, and he was no stranger to feeling void of life's goodness. Understandably, he learned early how to disconnect from family, comforts, and hope.

It had been nearly six years since Jason's mother had communicated with him; so in January 2019, I followed an instinct, did some sleuthing, and found his workplace on social media. After a ten-hour drive from Tullahoma, Tennessee, to Jacksonville, I arrived unsure of what situation awaited. He emerged from the tow shop to greet me dressed in a heavily soiled navy-blue mechanic's uniform looking noticeably unkempt. We both smiled, and his eyes, though weary, still sparkled with an innocence and warmth I remembered. Despite his struggles with homelessness and addiction, Jason always carried that sensitive, considerate gentleness about him.

The radiant sun warmed us as we reconnected, sharing childhood memories. He never married, had no kids, enjoyed construction work, and liked to fish. He was bashful, reserved, still almost like that ten-year-old during the summer of '83. Though our conversation was brief, it was reminiscent of carefree days roaming the fields of Tanner Hill. As we hugged goodbye and assured one another we'd stay in touch, I offered him to ride back to Tennessee or to New York. "I'm happy here," he declined, hardly convincing. We continued to stay in touch through occasional phone calls and messaging, bridging the gap that time had created.

Each September, my cousins gather on Amelia Island for leisure, laughter, and heartfelt bonds. We'd invite Jason, and while he seemed interested in joining us, he never did. In August 2022, I realized our last communication had been several months prior. But that was not unusual because that's how Jason lived—unreachable by choice. When he did not respond to our September invite, I began searching again. I messaged his social media friends asking if they had seen him. It was not until February 2023 that I received a late-night response: "He's dead. I think overdose."

Taken aback, I started making calls—including to the Jacksonville Sheriff's Office to again inquire about a welfare check on my cousin. Their instruction was surreal: "Call homicide and the morgue in the morning." Unsettled and unresolved, that is how the night was meant to conclude. As I stood in my foyer ready for bed, without thought, I just said "Jason, wherever you are, I'm here for you. Just let me know what I'm supposed to do."

The first thing I did the morning of February 10, 2023, was call UF Health Shands morgue. "We don't have his body yet. I recommend that you call Chaplain Cynthia." I quickly dialed her number with nervous anticipation, and as our voices connected over the phone, it felt from a divine dimension. Both Chaplain Cynthia and I were awestruck to speak. After asking how I was related to Jason, she stated that his identity had been confirmed through fingerprints and his driver's license. She then revealed his most selfless act—he was a registered organ donor.

The chaplain explained that after working on the church ceiling, Jason and his co-worker friend Derk headed outside. Jason then suffered a cardiac event beside Derk's truck. Despite heroic efforts to resuscitate him, it was Jason's special time to find a new direction. The chaplain then quickly stated that she had to call me back as the surgical team was already preparing him for the next step. She had to rush to tell them a family member had wondrously been located. Jason's body, once so heavily burdened, was recalibrating its compass to bring renewal to those in need.

This was not a coincidence. It was something more profound—a synchronicity, a perfect alignment, a divine intervention. In the chaplain's voice there was compassion and reassurance, as though she knew the weight of the news she carried. I learned Jason was in his final time of transition—brain dead. His body no longer sustaining life as we know it but preparing to give life to others. It was as though the universe had gently guided the three of us together to this point, weaving a connection between dimensions of existence that words fail to describe.

After sharing the heartbreaking and miraculous news with Jason's mother, I arranged last-minute flights for her and his sister to fly from New York to Jacksonville. I drove from Tennessee, picked them up from the airport, and went to say goodbye to Jason. With mixed emotions, I found myself grateful, grief-stricken, numb, and humbled.

As I had stood in my foyer that night speaking to Jason's unseen presence, I wasn't prepared for what would be asked of me from another realm. Undeniably, it all made perfect sense in a way that transcended logic. It wasn't simply an ending—it was a transformation, a redirection of his essence into something profound and life-giving. And I was called to action as a facilitator. Mysterious ways, indeed.

Later, upon quiet reflection, I asked Jason if he could tell me what I should understand most about his experience in human form and why he chose distance and numbness. The word "hopelessness" presented itself in my mind, knowing this was his tender, spiritual, honest, and almost human response. Hopelessness is a powerful word: an adjective summoning emotions of despair, suggesting absence, or even finality.

Jason's journey did not end in darkness. He was not alone. He trusted the camaraderie shared with his loyal friend Derk, who also came to say farewell. He was treated with respect and dignity by his hospital care teams. In those moments, pure love filled Jason's room. He was no longer burdened. His last act of kindness transformed the lives of five individuals and their families. His story was one of struggle and hopelessness. Through his final act, he gave a most precious gift of enduring legacy—a new dimension of himself carried forward in the lives of others for generations: the silver lining. Peace be with you, Jason. Your compass finally pointed you home.

Dancing Through the Rain

by Stan Watkins

I was born a Hoosier, to some degree I remain one to this day. An incident in 1973 involving a six-foot-two man in a blond bouffant wig, sequined turquoise dress, and matching spike high heels, helped me break my bond to my little hometown, taking a step toward becoming who I am today.

Small Midwestern towns are not bastions of excitement. At age twenty-three, boredom placed me in an after-hours bar and in the arms of the above-noted man. That summer, semipro football provided a welcome respite from my day-to-day malaise. One night, after a spirited football game and a long bus ride, my adventure was set in motion.

My teammates were a rowdy bunch, drinking and carousing heavily, especially after our victorious games. I had little in common with most of them, but a bond as athletes was formed.

"Hey, we've gotta celebrate," Foggy Allen announced as our bus arrived back in town.

Foggy didn't need a victory to celebrate. He was the oldest member of the squad and he'd been a close friend of my older brother when they were adolescents in the '50s. But Foggy remained an adolescent, his life a series of misfortunes that alcohol caused for much of it.

"It's after two. The only place open is Pigget's," Tom Mitchell, said.

Tom was an undersized, overly aggressive defensive back, who often became combative when he drank. "They're open all night."

"Pigget's it is!" Foggy ordered.

Pigget's was an after-hours joint. Located two hundred yards from an area known locally as "The Lines"—a notorious, but tolerated, red-light district along the Wabash River. Their proximity didn't hinder the bar's reputation or business.

During regular hours, Pigget's patrons were mostly Black. After last call at other bars, Pigget's changed complexion. White college students, home for the summer or holiday, looking for excitement, found their way across the tracks, as did patrons unready to end their evening.

Pigget's was also a favorite haunt of Ronny Stackhouse. Everyone in town recognized Ronny. Several evenings a week he strutted about town, gaudily clad in drag. He was 6' 2"; his height and girth made more imposing by a beehive, blond wig. Spike high heels complemented his outfits. It was anyone's guess how he supported himself, affording his garish wardrobe. It didn't seem to matter. In the evenings, in costume, he was confident, completely at ease with his choice of persona. He had to be admired for that.

Surprisingly, I wasn't having a bad time nursing a glass of Coca-Cola at the bar, my back to the crowded dance floor. I was wondering why I didn't come there more often. A tap on my shoulder interrupted my reflections. Turning, I found Foggy, already well into his cups for the evening.

"Stan, thersssh a lady who wants to dansh with you." He slurred—his tongue seemingly coated with glue. I had to focus to understand him, but I could tell he was up to something. Most of my teammates stood behind him, cat-that-swallowed-the-canary looks on their faces. Glancing about, I saw no lady who appeared interested in me.

"Foggy, I don't dance much." This was true. Dancing was something I wished I could do, but I was unsure of myself on the dance floor. Although my ego was fairly intact, for a twenty-three-year-old, I hesitated to take chances that could potentially result in embarrassment. I wasn't a risk taker, which had, to that point, held me back from achieving a greater personal potential or from moving on from my hometown.

"You can't insult her," Foggy cautioned. Then he leaned in, wagged his finger, and whispered, "Not here: not a good idea."

I recalled the police blotter stories and those fights I'd heard about In Pigget's

"She's right over h-he-here," Foggy stammered, pointing to a spot in the direction of my amused teammates.

The crowd parted like The Red Sea, with Foggy improvising as Moses. At the end of the divided rows stood Ronny Stackhouse, all two hundred fifty-five pounds of him, smiling, arms outstretched, beckoning me to the dance floor. He wore his signature wig, heels, and a fluorescent-green, sequined, skintight dress.

The crowd broke into raucous, rhythmic clapping, along with cheers and hoots of laughter. Chuck Berry's "Johnny B. Goode" twanged from the jukebox,

I don't remember moving from my bar stool to Ronny's waiting arms but, somewhere between the refrain about a log cabin made of wood and a guy who never learned to read and write, I found myself firmly clutched in his embrace. The crowd quickly formed a circle, leaving Ronny in control of the floor—and me. Sometimes the anticipation of something unpleasant is worse than the actual event. This wasn't one of those times.

I didn't need to worry about my lack of dancing proficiency. Ronny arranged the choreography, flipping and spinning me about the floor like a rag doll. I still marvel at how gracefully he moved in those heels. *Where did he find them in that size? Where was he five hours ago when I could have used him on a double team block.* His dance moves would've made him a finalist in any dance contest.

In the succeeding years, I've heard "Johnny B. Goode" numerous times. It's never been as drawn out as the two or three hours it seemed that night. While Ronny twirled me about the floor, Mr. Berry's chorus of "go Johnny, go," was drowned out by the crowd's chant of "Go *Ronny*, go."

The mind can take you to the oddest places at the strangest times. Spinning around that dance floor, hoping for any means of escape, my mind flashed to a summer day not long before. I was biking with a friend on country roads, miles from any shelter. An unexpected thunderstorm blew in and within ten minutes we were soaked down to our shoes and socks.

"Well," my friend called cheerily over his shoulder, "one good thing— we can't get any wetter!"

Dancing that night with Ronny I reached a similar saturation point with my level of embarrassment. I had a revelation. I suddenly understood that part of my reluctance in the past to dancing was my fear of failing and appearing foolish. This was the same hesitancy I had in taking risks. On the dance floor of that sleazy bar—a linebacker-sized transvestite spinning me about—I realized that, as far as appearing foolish went, I couldn't "get any wetter."

I think some of Ronny's self-confidence rubbed off on me that night. So, I let go and went with it. I laughed, allowing myself to be spun around the floor in a series of pirouettes. I pivoted about and even twirled Ronny in a series of rock 'n' roll turns. When the music stopped, I dipped Ronny Stackhouse until he was horizontal with the floor. Twirling him back to his feet, I bowed to the crowd as Ronny, holding my hand, did a flawless curtsey to thunderous cheers.

Less than a year later, I was offered a job in New York State. It was similar to positions I had been offered several times before—when I was less self-assured. This time, I took the risk and moved from my small Hoosier town, never to return except for visits. I'm certain some of the confidence I learned from Ronny Stackhouse that evening was an impetus to taking that risk.

Now I'm retired, having had a successful career and life. Since leaving town, I've never encountered any of the people from that night. But through the filter of time, I occasionally reflect on that evening; sometimes wincing as I recall my embarrassment. But more often I reflect on how that event helped me become the stronger person I am now. At those times, I silently thank Foggy, my other teammates, and most of all Ronny Stackhouse for giving me that moment on that dance floor. I thank them all for showing me how to take risks. I thank them for pushing me to overcome my apprehension of feeling embarrassed. I thank them all for showing me how to dance through the rain.

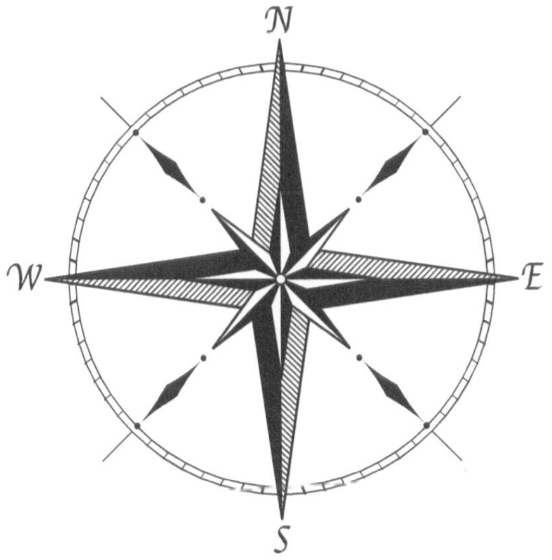

FICTION

The Pandemic

by Lynn Bechdolt

I t's just a cold, Charlotte thought, with a tickle in her throat. By day's end, her throat and her lungs hurt, especially when she coughed. She called her neighbor, each of them comparing symptoms and deciding to wait until morning. She woke in the morning when her lungs burned, gasping for breath, and coughing—a sign of the "lung-eating" virus.

The medic loaded her into the ambulance and said, "University Trauma, ASAP."

At the hospital, she had vague memories of people calling out, "Heart rate ninety, oxygen eighty-nine percent and dropping," then ". . . anesthesia and intubation."

She drifted away.

Sometime later, she gradually woke up in a gently lit room with no tubes or machines. She couldn't raise her head, then realized she was wrapped in a warm cocoon. The walls were medium beige, like every hospital. That's where she was!

"Mrs. Hanson, are you awake?" a bodiless voice whispered in her ears.

"What? Who is this?"

"You're in the hospital. We're very glad you're awake now. We'll be in shortly."

"Wait, nobody's here. How can you be talking to me in my head?"

"You have tiny devices in your ears for messages."

"Messages? What does that mean?"

In a few minutes, two people in hazmat suits arrived and removed her wrappings. Her once floppy arms looked like skin stretched over scrawny muscle and bone.

"Why are you dressed in suits? Am I infectious?"

One of the men smiled. "No, ma'am, *you* aren't infectious. We just don't want to expose you to what *we* might have. You've been under for a while, a long while. So, you don't have the immunity we have."

She was startled, but he was gone before she could ask him what he meant. How long had she been sick or in a coma? She was comfortable, not hungry nor sleepy. She had to concentrate, but her fingers and toes slowly began to move willingly.

A young woman limped into the room in a white coat; a name stitched on it.

She smiled and said, "I'm glad to see you're moving on your own. We'll be doing a lot more of that to get you ready to leave. Do you remember me, Grandma?"

Charlotte stared at her for a minute. "Emma? But you just graduated from high school!"

She took her grandmother's hand. "You've been in a medically induced coma for ten years. You're very important. After they put you on the ventilator, they discovered your lungs were in tatters and you're an AB-blood type. Nobody could give you a lung transplant. Despite all that, your antibodies fought back, just very slowly. They are antibodies that don't lose effectiveness over time.

"The university, with Uncle Rick's consent, periodically harvested your antibodies, which the hospital did every so often. Your antibodies were sent around the world and saved thousands of lives, including mine, although my left foot didn't heal completely. I lost some toes.

"In the meantime, we discovered that your lung tissue was growing back very, very slowly. But it was completely immune to that whole family of lung viruses.

"First, we asked you every few months: did you want to give more cells? You kept saying 'Yes.' Finally, you said, 'Don't bother. Take as much as you can. I'll be okay.' So, they kept taking some of your cells, which slowed down your progress. They studied how your body was making more cells. Whenever we tried to bring you out of coma, your lungs stopped repairing themselves. So, here you are, finally awake with lungs like a newborn baby. That makes you the heroine of our time.

"By the way, Grandma, we are billionaires, the whole family, from all the research and drugs your body produced. This hospital is twice as big now and it's called the Hanson Research and Trauma Center."

Two weeks later, Charlotte was wheeled out the front door of the hospital. She didn't know what to think when she saw the crowd. At least a hundred people were cheering her and waving signs that said We're Here Becuz of U while tiny flying cameras moved like bumblebees between the crowd and her.

A young woman shouted at her, "Thank you, Mrs. Hanson!" and blew her a kiss.

"What happened to you?"

The woman jumped up and down. "I couldn't breathe. My lungs were dying and your cells healed me!"

The hospital director standing next to her touched a microphone at his throat. "People, *yes*, this is the *woman* who made our present lives possible." His voice echoed through the sound system. "We learned from her and other AB-negative people how to tailor antibodies to fight lung viruses for people of other blood types. Then we learned from her how to generate rapid healing from damaged vital organs as her sleeping body healed itself. Now, let's hear it for Charlotte Hanson, the great giver!"

The crowd roared, tossed confetti, and blew horns.

"Ricky, who are all these people?"

"They are people who were healed by medicine developed from your cells, Mom. Right here in this hospital."

Her son Rick helped her into an aircar, something she had never seen before. As the car rose over the hospital, she spied a building she knew.

"Ricky, why are the Diamond Towers empty? Some of the window-panes are broken, and no one's moving around in there. That used to be the poshest place to work in the whole city."

Her son patted her hand. "Lots of people died, Mom. Especially those who worked in the downtown areas where the air pollution concentrated because of the traffic."

She held her son's hand as she looked out the window, noticing the vacant places where houses and businesses once stood. She turned to him. "Emma told me I'm a billionaire. That I own part of the hospital. How can that be?"

He couldn't contain a grin. "You know me, Mom, I cut a deal. I permitted them to use your body tissues as long as you weren't getting sicker. When they asked about your strong antibodies, I let them take samples, but our family kept the rights to any medicines or treatments developed from them. Your antibodies worked amazingly well. So, I signed a contract that said we would get fifty cents for every dose they made, five cents of which would go to support more research at the University Trauma Center. They made three *billion* doses and they are still making more.

"Finally, I told them to stop and let you heal, which took a long time. Now, we're going out to ten square miles of our own family farm."

"How many people did I help?"

"Millions. Anybody with the lung virus we could reach, Mom. That's why I let them."

On the trip to her new home, she held her son's hand and looked down on the countryside, squeezing his hand as hard as she could while her tears flowed. "I never thought I was generous. When you were growing up, I was the one who pinched pennies. We had to, but your father was more generous than I was." She turned to him. "I'm glad you turned out to be more like him."

"Mom, it was both of you."

Secrets of the Forest

by Barbara A. Busenbark

The rhythmic sound of Smokey's hooves on the pavement softened when she stepped onto the dirt trail. A river of fallen leaves crunched like potato chips underneath each step. The smell of her leather saddle mingled with the clean, brisk air. The beech branches refused to let go of their leaves until winter made it impossible to hold on.

It is on such days the woods reveal their secrets. In winter, snow drifts hide the past. In summer, trees massed with leaves shroud the view. It is in the nakedness of late autumn that we can see what may have been.

In that barren state, a fieldstone foundation emerged in the distance during my ride. From where I sat, I couldn't tell what had been there. I didn't know if some calamity destroyed a home or maybe a barn.

A rustle of leaves deep in the woods caught my attention. I turned in my saddle hoping to catch sight of a deer or frolicking squirrels. Another glimpse through the trees and the abandoned foundation no longer stood derelict. A branch appeared to point toward a cabin surrounded by a hazy blur with an orange hue. I noticed the scent of burning wood and saw a ribbon of smoke streaming from the chimney. The bright-blue sky turned gray.

Silence followed, and an unnatural quiet consumed the woods. No birds chirped or acorns dropped. A cool breeze swept across my face causing my eyes to blur. I strained to focus.

Smokey froze. Her nostrils flared and her ears swiveled in the direction of the cabin. Her body stiffened beneath me. I feared she would bolt. I looked down to grab the saddle horn. A flowing dress had replaced the blue jeans I put on before my ride. Voices in the distance pierced the stillness.

Two children, dressed in colonial garb, came running toward us.

"Please help, it's Mother, she's ill," the boy called out.

"Please," begged his sister.

I climbed down from Smokey and tied her reins to a tree. I too wore clothes from another time. The emergency at hand tempered my confusion. I grabbed hold of my skirt and rushed after the children. The abandoned foundation now supported a simple house.

The boy flung open the door. A woman under a patchwork quilt lay on a bed. As I approached her, she reached out her hand.

"Helen, I'm so glad you're here."

"Sadie, is it the baby?" The words came from my mouth, but I didn't understand how I knew her name or condition.

"Yes, and it's too soon. Fetch Doctor Trowbridge. Please hurry."

"You hold on Sadie; I'll be back as soon as I can. Children, go fetch some water for your mother; I'll be back soon."

With that, I raced back to Smokey and hoisted myself into the saddle. She seemed to sense the urgency. I turned her around and down the trail we cantered. When we got to the end of the trail, Smokey leapt over the drainage gully and onto the pavement. *Pavement?*

"Whoa girl," I called out, pulling on the reins. I looked down. Once again, I was wearing jeans. The mystical haze dissipated. We slowed to a walk as I tried to gather my thoughts. *What just happened? Was I in another dimension?* Everything around me turned familiar again. My head spun with confusion, conjecture and then calm. I needed to get a grip on myself, think through what had happened.

When I reached home, I climbed down off Smokey and unbuckled her cinch. As I went to work sliding her saddle off, I thought, *should I tell my husband what happened? Would he think I'd lost my mind?*

I deposited the tack in the barn, just as I did after every ride. Continuing on as though nothing strange had happened, I separated a couple of flakes of hay to put in the rack on the side of the barn.

"How was your ride, Helen?" Jim called out.

Startled by the interruption of my swirling thoughts, I quickly answered, "It was great . . . beautiful day." In that instant I decided to keep my experience to myself. At least until I figured it out.

"By the way, Jon went over to Carl's, and Sarah went shopping with the Rumsons."

"Thanks, hun, a little time to ourselves."

During the week for the next month, I spent my lunch hour in the town library's reference room.

"Can I help you find something?" Anne, the research librarian, asked.

"Hi Anne, where can I find the old town reports?"

"Right this way. They are bound in ten-year increments, dating back to 1787 when they first started documenting town records. Is there something in particular I can help you find?"

"No, thank you." *How could I tell her I was looking for a record of a ghost?*

The annual reports documented the births, deaths, marriages, property taxes, and budgets. Incidental information often provided interesting tidbits about daily life. Things like "John Menard's cows got loose and had to be penned next to the town house until he fixed his fence." "Amy Grant's sister moved to Boston." "The new minister will arrive in Spring." Sometimes I got caught up reading such minutia.

On the weekends, I rode the same trail. The fieldstone foundation that supported Sadie's house remained steadfast and silent, refusing to give up any more clues. The days grew shorter and colder. The ground hardened during the frosty nights. Still, I rode unwilling to forget what happened.

The cycle of research during the weeks and riding on the weekend to try and solve a mystery that I didn't want to share grew tiresome. Anne and I exchanged pleasantries with each visit.

"You are determined; I'm here if you need anything," Anne would say.

"Just doing a little research, thanks."

"You know the selectmen are looking for a local historian to sort through the records we boxed up during the town hall's renovation. If you're interested, I could put in a good word for you. They are hoping to make the town's history more accessible."

"Let me think about it; I might just take you up on that."

I couldn't quit my searching. It became an addiction. An urge that wouldn't let go. Page after page, year after year, decade after decade, I continued my quest. It was as though Sadie continued to speak to me.

Another weekend came and went. On Monday's lunch break, I told Anne of my interest in the position of town historian.

"The job is yours for the taking; my husband is on the board of selectmen. I told him about you, and he loved the idea."

As I made my way to the reference room, I realized my life was headed in an entirely new direction. No longer confined to my cubicle processing forms at the bank, this was a job I could enjoy. I looked at the volumes of reports with renewed vigor.

My time spent in the reference room felt like time travel. The room itself contained remnants of the town's past. With over one hundred years of additions to the library, the reference room stood as the original building dating back to the 1890s. Above the time-darkened shelves stern faced portraits of library benefactors looked down upon patrons. Tables surrounded by vintage Windsor chairs occupied the oak floor. A stately grandfather wall clock hung above a simple but elegant mantlepiece. The clock no longer chimed, and the fireplace remained cold.

I stepped away from the table and walked around the room looking at the gentlemen in the gold-leaf frames. Each one had a brass plaque: Rev. Abeil Abbot, 1802-1868, followed by George S. Morrison1820-1880, next Dr. Daniel Trowbridge, 1832-1900. Staring right at me—Dr. Trowbridge. *Was he Sadie's Dr. Trowbridge?*

I reached for the volume titled *Smithfield Town Reports 1880-1890*. As my lunch hour closed in on me, I frantically looked through the death records. "Sadie Sawyer and baby girl, October 12, 1888." *The same day I rode into the woods. I couldn't save her*. An asterisk beside her name jumped out at me.

"*Helen Roberts took in the widow Sawyer's two other children, Jonathan and Sarah."

Maisie

by Scott Corey

First came radical political change, then defiance, armed rebellion, cries for separation, the great population migration, dissolution of the American Dream, and finally, open warfare. With the dissolution and warfare came the breakdown of modernization.

June, 2085

On the border between the United Federation and the North American Alliance.

Maisie Walcott felt sick watching her sister clean the sniper rifle. Seated on the plank-board porch in the summer twilight, she watched Eva disassemble the weapon and wipe each part with a rag. *She loves that sniper rifle more than she loves her family,* Maisie thought. *Certainly more than she loves me.*

Eva wore a black beret of the Defense Force. She joined a year ago when she turned nineteen. Sometimes Maisie wanted to shout at her to stop because she was sick of it. Always the shooting and death.

Her father sat slumped in a wheelchair, taking in his slow breaths with a subtle, cancerous rasp. She patted his arm tenderly beneath the thin blanket.

"Should I take him in?" she asked as her mother came from the kitchen.

"Not quite yet, honey," her mother replied, dropping onto a chair, and propping her legs on the low porch table. "I need a break myself."

"I'll do it," Eva replied. "I'm almost finished here."

Maisie was a year younger than Eva. Their brother Darnell was fifteen. He came out the screen door. They had heard him tromping down the stairs.

"Look here," he said with a grin. "Whole family watching Eva clean her rifle."

"Shut up," Eva said. She and Darnell didn't get along. Being the eldest and the most aggressive in the family, Eva thought of her younger brother as foolishly silly.

"Now, Eva," their mother said.

Someone clapped at the gate. It was Jamie, Eva's boyfriend. He was also in the Defense Force.

"Get that weapon nice and clean," he said to Eva. "We got Naals to kill tomorrow."

Naals was their term for citizens of the North American Alliance, the country across the river.

"You shut up too," Eva snapped.

He laughed. "C'mon."

Eva put away her rifle and looked at her mother and sister questioningly.

"Don't worry," Maisie said. "I'll help Papa."

Eva nodded and went through the gate with Jamie.

Maisie heard cicadas in the trees and watched a firefly twinkling across the yard. The mosquitoes would be out soon. Getting up from her place on the porch, she wheeled her father into the house.

———

The next morning, Maisie walked out to the back stoop. She loved this time of day, when the world was fresh and full of promise. Each morning when she rose from the blankets and gazed outside, it seemed the world had refreshed itself and life could start anew and be better than before.

A goldfinch swooped down from a maple tree by the fence and winged up again. Maisie studied him, loving the lemon yellow of his feathers. Eva came outside and stood beside her, taking in a deep breath of the cool morning air. As she zipped up her camouflaged hood, she glanced at the white flour on Maisie's hands. For her, revenge was the purpose of life. Eva didn't want to kill just one Naal shooter; she wanted to kill them all. She wouldn't be happy until she put a bullet in the head of the last enemy. So now, standing in the cool morning air, she looked smugly at Maisie for staying home and making breakfast.

"You're weak," Eva said. "And too sensitive. Where would our world be if everyone was like you?"

"Maybe better," Maisie replied and brushed the flour from her hands. She didn't think of herself as weak. She had a different way of looking at things, but this didn't mean her ideas were wrong. She stepped back into the kitchen. Her mother stood there with a bucket.

"Need you to pick me some blackberries," she said. "Gonna make a cobbler today."

"All right," Maisie said, taking off her apron.

"That patch west of the Davis place is ripe . . . and safe."

There was always a danger of being shot if you got too close to the riverbank. The Naal snipers across the river were relentless.

Grabbing the bucket, Maisie cut through a gap in the fence and took a dirt path through the apple orchard. As she passed the pond, a grasshopper fluttered over the water's surface and a trout got him. Maisie watched the circular green ripples from where the trout came out of the water. It happened just that fast. One second the grasshopper was there, and the next it was in a trout's belly. From life to death in a snap of the fingers. She wondered if it happened that fast for shooters on the riverbank. One moment you were camouflaged and waiting for a shot, and the next, you were in Heaven.

A sandstone bluff shielded the blackberry patch from the river. The dark berries stained Maisie's fingertips as she picked her way among the bushes. When the bucket was full, she hiked through the pines to the top of the bluff. From here, lying flat, she peered down at the river. It was so wide and beautiful, she felt it put her life in perspective. The river had been here for thousands of years and would still be here in thousands more, if the river Jordan were still flowing . . .

Below her, a thick blackberry patch grew on the riverbank.

I should go down there. Eva has me afraid of my own shadow. Why would anyone want to harm me? If I stood up now and waved, bet no one would care.

Pressing her face to the sandy earth, she scooched down the incline. A wild thought occurred to her, and she walked around the bluff to the water's edge. She had never been this close to the river before. It was exciting. Kneeling, she touched the cold water.

"Maisie!" a voice cried. "What're you doing? Get down!"

It was Eva. She had settled into a shooting position beneath a fallen oak tree. Amid the broken tree limbs and with her camouflaged hood, she blended in so well, Maisie hadn't seen her.

"Get down!" Eva shouted again.

A muted *phutt* sounded from beneath the fallen oak. Eva had fired off a round at the far bank. The *phutt* sound came from the silencer on her rifle.

Shading her eyes, Maisie gazed across the expanse of water to a tree line on the far bank. It was a pleasant June morning with a cool breeze coming off the water. For someone over there, Eva might've made it their last morning. Maybe they were lying in the weeds now, gazing up at the cloudless, royal-blue sky and thinking how they would miss the sunshine. Or perhaps they weren't thinking at all.

Just like that. The trout takes the grasshopper.

Maisie picked a handful of berries. They were sweet, perhaps even sweeter than the berries behind the bluff. But the hair on the back of her neck stood up, and fear gripped her. She wasn't ready to die, especially to prove a point about the Naals. Keeping low, she scrambled up the riverbank and around the pond to the apple orchard. Slipping through the gap in the fence, she stepped up to the porch.

"That you, Maisie?" her mother called.

"Yes," she replied.

Her mother glanced at the bucket approvingly.

"Rinse them off in the sink. Get going now."

When she was baking, her mother didn't like to be kept waiting.

Maisie went inside.

Across the river, Trace Dewey lowered his sniper rifle. A girl had been picking berries by the water's edge. She wore a loose-fitting gingham summer dress and carried a red plastic bucket. She looked about his age. He couldn't imagine what she was thinking, exposing herself so openly.

His sights focused on her temple. The hollow-point shell would go in small and come out like a squashed melon. He touched his finger to the trigger and hesitated. It felt wrong to kill a young woman for picking berries, even if she lived in the United Federation. Climbing down from his maple-tree perch, Trace crouched and headed through the marsh grass toward home.

He wouldn't tell anybody.

Moon Dreams

by L.H. Davis

Needing to save enough oxygen for the return trip, Bryan decided to turn back if he saw nothing from the crest of the next hill.

"Yes!" he said, spotting the debris field of the Apollo 12 Lunar Lander. The actual landing site was too far away, but he was confident a photo of the ascent stage wreckage would impress the kids in his class.

But . . . what is that?

A transparent spacecraft with a thirty-foot spherical hull sat among the debris. A pair of astronauts stood outside the ship. They were facing him but looking down. Not knowing which radio channel they used, Bryan tried them all.

"Hello? Hello?" And then they looked up.

The taller one waved. "Hello. Please remain calm," he said in a thick foreign accent. "We won't harm you."

"What do you mean?" Bryan said, bouncing closer.

The man took a step to his right—and to his left—with a pair of hind legs.

Bryan froze—mouth open.

"We *are* friendly . . . just not human. I'm Gortha. This is my daughter, Zarah."

The female nodded as her rear legs stepped out from behind her and curtsied.

"What's your name?" Gortha asked.

"Bry— Bryan. What are you?"

"I'm an anthropologist. Zarah is studying to be an engineer."

"A mechanical engineer," she said.

"But— *What* are you?"

"That's complicated. You wouldn't be able to pronounce the name of our species but, long ago, humans called us Centaurs."

"The mythological creature that was part human and part horse?"

"Yes, although we're not a mixture of anything. We simply have four legs and two arms, not unlike your own."

Zarah turned sideways exposing her full length, then walked her rear around to face Bryan. "We don't have horse fur or tails, either."

"When we first visited Earth," Gortha said, "humans were not quite ready to meet space travelers. Of course, the fact we had to wear pressure suits complicated things."

Bryan nodded. "Why did you have to wear pressure suits on Earth?"

Zarah giggled. "We don't breathe oxygen."

"Like you," Gortha said, "we breathe mostly nitrogen, but instead of oxygen, we need a mixture of methane. Oxygen is rare in this galaxy, but methane is everywhere."

"Not on Earth's moon. Where do you live?"

Gortha shrugged. "We have a base on Titan, Saturn's largest moon."

Zarah stepped closer. "I've never seen a human up close. Do you mind?"

"No." Bryan stepped forward.

The clear bubbles of their helmets clunked together.

Her pupils were like a cat's, tall and narrow, surrounded by greenish-gold. She appeared to be hairless, with a subtle green sheen to her skin. The shape of her face seemed quite human, although her lips were larger than most, plump, and sky blue.

She's my age. Bryan grinned. "Your lips are pretty blue."

"Do you mean *very* blue . . . or beautiful?"

"Beautiful."

"Thank you. I sometimes wear red lipstick, like human women."

"Is that blue lipstick?"

"No, that's me. I like your brown eyes. They're cute."

Bryan flushed.

"Your cheeks turned red. Can you turn other colors?"

"Not on purpose. Why are you here . . . on Earth's moon?"

"It's my birthday, so Daddy's showing me the artifacts humans have left here over the years. I like exploring."

"Me too, only I have to walk. You're lucky to have your own ship."

"I guess . . . but we also have a problem."

"Two, actually," Gortha said. "You . . . and a dead battery."

Wide-eyed, Bryan said, "Me?"

Gortha nodded. "You shouldn't know we even exist or about our base on Titan."

"Daddy, they're going to find out soon anyway. That's why they're here."

Bryan frowned. "You know about the ship we're building to go to Saturn?"

Gortha laughed. "It's my job to know. Our mission is to study humans."

"Am I in trouble?" Bryan asked.

"No," Gortha said. "We're the ones in trouble. We just came from the Apollo 12 landing site, and you-know-who opened an old nuclear power supply."

Zarah stomped her foot. "I said I was sorry. How was I supposed to know what was inside?"

"It's actually my fault," Gortha said. "I left the ship's hatch open. Had I closed it, the ship would have been shielded. The dose was small, and our suits warned us in time, but the command console took a direct hit. The radiation ruined the battery that powers the electronics and both backup batteries. When I shut down the engine here, that was it. We can't power up the computer to restart the ship."

"We have batteries back at the lunar base. What size do you need?"

"I can attach bare wires to any battery," Zarah said, "as long as it produces something near the right—What's your word?—Voltage!"

"Is it a big battery? Or is it small, like in my flashlight?" He unclipped it from his belt.

Gortha turned and reached inside the open hatch. Discarding two of the old, shiny batteries, which formed small craters in the lunar dust, he held out a third. It was half the size of the flashlight.

Bryan took it and studied the strange writing on the side. Recognizing nothing, he shrugged and unscrewed the bottom of his flashlight. Removing the battery, he placed it and the dead one in Gortha's open palm.

Zarah snagged both batteries, discarding the dead one as she climbed inside the ship.

Bryan watched her work through the transparent hull.

Removing a meter with probes from a cabinet, she straddled one of the odd pilot seats. Resting on her chest and stomach, she placed Bryan's battery and a meter on the bench. After adjusting the meter, she touched the probes to the ends of the battery.

She shook her head. "Not enough. Only about half of what we need."

Bryan knew the battery in his suit was higher voltage, and he had a spare, but his *life* depended on them. And if he went back to base with a battery missing, he'd be in serious trouble.

What have I gotten myself into? I just wanted to take a picture—The camera battery!

"Try this one," Bryan said, unclipping the camera from his belt. Flipping open the bottom, he released the battery. "It's smaller but higher voltage to handle the electronics."

Zarah engaged the probes . . . and squealed. "Yes! Can we borrow it?"

Bryan grinned. "Sure. You can have it. I've got a spare at home. Is it big enough to get you back to Saturn?"

"It only needs to boot the computer," Gortha said. "We fold space, so we'll be home in a matter of seconds." Pulling up, he climbed inside, front legs first, then rear.

Zarah fused wires to the terminals and then flipped a switch on the console, which flickered to life. She smiled and met Bryan's eyes as she stood. Bryan stepped up to the open hatch.

Zarah reached out and cradled his helmet in her hands. "I wish we didn't have to wear these stupid helmets."

Bryan felt heat rising in his cheeks. "We can hold our breaths and take them off."

She laughed. "No, we can't, and you know it . . . but I do wish we could."

"Me too. We can *pretend* we did."

Zarah smiled shyly. "I will if you will."

"It's a deal."

Gortha chuckled. "Nice meeting you, Bryan, and thanks for the help. Maybe we'll see you on Titan one day."

"Count on it!"

"Watch your head," Gortha said as the hatch came down.

Bryan stepped back a few feet and watched through the hull as Zarah settled onto her seat. After she strapped in, the ground beneath his boots began to vibrate. Gortha met his eyes, smiled, and nodded to the side; so Bryan stepped farther back. As Zarah waved, the ship disappeared.

For a moment, Bryan gazed out over the ancient ascent stage debris field. Raising his camera, he groaned, "No battery." Disappointed, he bowed his head, and his eyes were drawn to Zarah's boot prints in the dust. He squatted, touching one of the depressions with his gloved finger.

I wonder if she has a boyfriend?

A glint of silver appeared beneath his fingertip. Clearing away the dust, he uncovered a shiny battery with strange writing.

"Yes! One of the Centaur batteries! Best show-and-tell ever!"

An Unlikely Superhero

by Nanette Davis

I hadn't planned to be anybody's superhero, but the moment I spotted Barney something changed in me.

The poor dog had been locked in a small cage at the local shelter. He had patiently watched the sights and smelled the scents. Through the bars he had seen other fur babies released to forever homes, but he was not one of them.

What was I thinking? I had just been diagnosed with Stage-4 pancreatic cancer. I felt like a failure. My future was uncertain, and I barely had enough money to feed myself, let alone a pet! I filled out adoption paperwork anyway and lied to the manager about my financial status. I handed over a check that would bounce before noon, then stumbled out of the shelter with Barney. We stood on the corner, breathing.

Barney made several pee-pee stops before we arrived at my apartment. I spread out an old blanket in the room and encouraged my new friend to sit. I searched the kitchen for a clean bowl, filled it with water, and set down a dish of Rice Chex for him.

"A growing boy has gotta eat." I reached over to stroke his back.

It was a newbie dog owner no-no. Sweet Barney chomped down hard on my finger, and I felt twinges in my toes. Blood dripped onto the kitchen tile.

"Damn you, dog!" I rinsed off my wound, and thoughts spun in my head of typhoid and rabies. My oncologist warned me to be careful and to avoid infection risks. I scoured my medicine cabinet for an antiseptic.

I heard a whimper. There stood Barney, his ears flat against his skull, trembling, gazing up at me with fearful eyes.

"Why?" I asked. "I was just trying to be nice to you." He tilted his head.

The weeks went by. Barney and I became closer. I enjoyed our walks, watching his little nose twitching at every odor. He allowed me to cuddle him.

During my chemo treatments, I barely left the couch. As the cuckoo clock ticked away the hours, Barney kept me warm through those chilly nights. In the mornings, he woke me by licking my face. At breakfast time, he raced around the kitchen in anticipation until I set down his bowl. Then he would thank me with a happy howl. On my better days, we played fetch. I loved watching his champagne fur blowing in the wind.

After two months sharing my couch, I knew time was precious. Barney and I went for a hike in the woods. As soon as I let him off of his lead, he ran around, spinning like a whirlwind. Every cell of his body was relishing this long-awaited freedom. A warm sensation came over me as I watched him. I felt happiness for the first time in ages. Was this fifteen-pound fur ball giving me hope for the future? I choked back tears. My latest CT Scan results proved hope was futile.

We skipped down the trail toward a picturesque pond. Barney spotted the swans and he went charging into the water. He doggy paddled in circles. The swans paid little attention to him, but they honked at me because I was laughing so loudly. When Barney seemed tired, I whistled for him to come ashore. He trotted toward me. His fur, now soaked and matted, had caused his legs to appear half their size. He rolled around in the grass.

That night as I snuggled under the covers, I took one last glance at my boy. His eyes were twitching back and forth under his eyelids. I dreamt of swans and fresh air. We slept soundly.

As my cuckoo clock chimed each hour, my body was failing at an alarming rate. With each tick and step, I was lurching toward my fate. I no longer felt hungry, so I gave my food to Barney. My frequent and painful trips to the bathroom were taking a huge toll, and not just for me. Some days I had to rely on doggie pads, since I had little energy to walk Barney.

One day I noticed my pup dragging his left rear foot. He was no longer holding his head up. His eyes were distant. Knowing he was already twelve years old, I managed to scrape up enough change for a taxi to get him to the vet.

She said, "Your dog was infected by a parasite, most likely acquired from pond water. The infection may have reached his brain. I'm afraid there's no cure. Take him home and watch for signs of deterioration."

I heard every word, but my heart refused to believe. Barney had survived those lonely years in a shelter. Was this his reward? A fatal parasite from his first ever romp in the woods?

That evening, I made six trips to the bathroom, and I couldn't stand straight due to the pain. My chemo treatments were not working. It was only a matter of time. Barney gazed up at me. He nuzzled into my side. I stroked my finger through his fur. "It's okay, boy. We've got each other."

As I dozed off, I thought I heard music. I wasn't sure where it was coming from, but the beautiful sound lulled me into a deep slumber. I felt my hand on Barney's soft fur. Then I heard a whisper.

"I was waiting for you my whole life. Whenever anyone looked at me, it was always no, not him. I lay in that cage for so long, dreaming of the moment when a loving human would appreciate my champagne fur, hold me and make me feel wanted. We had fun paddling around the cool pond water. Those swans were beautiful. I love you Devin, but I am feeling so sleepy. It hurts to stay awake."

Was this all just a fuzzy dream? The clock stopped ticking. I felt Barney's paw receding. Then I saw a light off in the distance. Barney and I were running free in a beautiful field.

Ordenado Park

by Diana Faherty

It gets loud early in the apartment, right as the sun is starting to light the sky. Pots and pans clatter in the kitchen and adult voices continue the arguments laid to rest at bedtime last night. Georgie pulls the pillow over his head and turns toward the wall, except his younger brother Miguel is wedged in there.

"Aww shoot." Georgie gives up trying to get back to sleep and tumbles out of bed, then heads for the bathroom. Except Tia Louisa is in there. And two of his cousins are lined up waiting their turn.

I really have to go, Georgie thinks, then remembers the park down the street has public restrooms. Georgie slides into his flipflops, throws on a thin T-shirt, and slips out the front door. He trudges down the sidewalk through the cool and quiet, all eight years and forty-eight inches of him.

It's his second day in this new place. His family arrived at the Casa Verde Apartments Friday night, and his aunt and uncle insisted the exhausted family take one of the bedrooms. It's just him and Miguel and Mami and Papi now that his older brother, Javier, left a few weeks ago. They're sharing this apartment with two other families.

Georgie lets himself into the men's bathroom, and when he's done he washes his hands and puts the paper towel in the trash can. There's a lot of trash on the floor, so he picks all of that up too. Mami always told him to keep things clean because cleanliness is next to godliness. And he wants to go to Heaven.

"Boy, people don't care about this place," Georgie mutters as he walks past the twisted swing sets and sticky concrete picnic tables on his way back to the apartment. He shuffles through fast-food wrappers and kicks empty beer bottles out of his way. *Eww, there's a baby diaper . . . and a sodden T-shirt. Is that a hypodermic needle and a condom?* Oh yes, he knows what those are. Before he disappeared, Javier made sure Georgie understood some of the bad things he'd run into in the world. Georgie carefully picks up the needle and the condom and deposits them in the garbage can at the entrance to the park.

Going to the bathroom at the park becomes a morning routine for Georgie—beats waiting an hour to get into the bathroom at the apartment. Georgie always takes a garbage bag with him to collect trash. The first time it took only ten minutes to fill up the thirteen-gallon bag, and the park didn't look any cleaner. Beer cans, broken strollers, lawn mower parts, discarded towels, more diapers. But now, a couple weeks later, things are looking much better and it takes him awhile to fill his bag.

One afternoon, on his way home from school, he sees a bent-over man in a dirty white T-shirt and baggy jeans picking up trash at the park. "I seen you do this in the morning and figgered I could do some good too," he tells Georgie. "Gotta keep it clean for the young'uns."

The man's name is Amos, and he sleeps in the park sometimes. He's missing teeth at the top and bottom of his mouth. His greasy hair is pulled back into a tiny ponytail, and tobacco juice stains his beard. He admits he's responsible for some of the trash, but he's going to start picking it up, he tells Georgie. He likes to talk about his wife, now dead, and the house they used to own not far from here. "She made the best sweet potato pie. Usta sell ten pies a day outta our house." He smacks his lips and looks toward the sky. "The good Lord took her and then the taxman took our house. This park is like home to me now."

Georgie starts making friends with other regulars at the park. One of his favorites is Bridgett, who comes with her baby girl to sit on the swings. You wouldn't know it from her bright-orange hair and giant eyelashes, but she's very studious, putting herself through nursing school. She comes to the park after classes and before heading to her grandmother's house to fix dinner for the old woman. Bridgett works the overnight shift at the 7-Eleven down the street, and Georgie enjoys hearing her stories about the people who stop in, like the man who always adds coffee to his Slurpee or the lady who lost her acrylic nail on the hot dog grill. Bridgett always finds humor in life.

Officer Brown is the neighborhood policeman who cruises by every couple of hours. The first time he stopped his police car beside Georgie to ask him questions, the boy was terrified— afraid this cop would take him to jail or tell him to get out of the park. Trusting cops doesn't come easily to Georgie's family, not after they came for Javier. But the day Officer Brown gives him a Spider Boy comic book, Georgie decides he's okay. Officer Brown starts walking through the park instead of driving by. He high-fives the kids. Some afternoons he'll walk with Georgie on his way home from school, asking about his teachers and what he's learning. Georgie welcomes these talks because, when he gets home, there's no one at the apartment to tell about his day.

Georgie introduces Officer Brown to the old men who play dominoes in the park. At first, they would hide their bottles wrapped up in paper bags, but Officer Brown said it looks like they're just drinking soda and, as long as they don't get noisy or start fighting, the old men can go on drinking whatever is in those bottles. Georgie likes sitting with the men and listening to the clacking of the dominoes on the table. Sometimes the men will ask Georgie to add up the board count for them. That helps him learn his numbers.

After school, Georgie starts bringing some of his classmates to the park. They play dodgeball and catch, then end up doing a sweep through the park to pick up trash. The park has never looked better. It has greened up, and everything seems to shine. The dominoes men decide to rename the park. "Ordenado Park," one man declares. "Tidy and orderly."

Amos disappears for a while, and Georgie misses him and his stories about the old days. One day Georgie sees Officer Brown walking toward him with a thin man by his side. Is it …? Could that be Amos? It *is* Amos, wearing a custodian's coveralls with his hair cut short and minus his beard. "I got me a job at Casa Verde," he tells Georgie. Now he has a place to sleep.

One afternoon as he's walking home through the park, Georgie sees some SUVs pull up outside his apartment. Men in blue jackets with the letters I-C-E on the back stream out and enter the building. Georgie's head starts to pound and he finds it hard to breathe. Visions of these men carrying Javier away race through his head. His parents had warned him this might happen and, if he ever saw these men again, he should run away and hide. Georgie starts to turn and runs smack into Officer Brown.

"Don't worry, Georgie," the policeman says, placing protective hands on the boy's shoulders. "I made sure nobody's home. And I found a new place for you and your family to live. Let me take you there. We're sure going to miss you. You made a real difference here."

The Midnight Gardener

by Cristina Farinas

Sylvie ate her bowl of cereal standing at the kitchen sink. Through the window, she saw her barren property—lifeless dirt, two spindly slash pines, Orlando's smog hanging thick. It hadn't rained in weeks, but even if it had, she'd long since given up on the garden. Once, she had dreamed of a backyard sanctuary where she could draw and paint, but both dreams had withered, buried under the weight of practicality and expectations.

She rinsed her bowl and placed it in the dishwasher. It was Thursday—dishwashing night. Friday was for washing her hair. Saturdays, a movie. Sundays, cleaning and meal prep. Meatloaf on Mondays, tacos on Tuesdays, leftovers Wednesdays. Baked chicken, fish, takeout—every week, the same. Ordered, predictable, like her job. Like her life.

At precisely 8:30 every morning, Sylvie arrived at the office. If early, she waited by the door. She was never late. She spent mornings on emails, invoices, reports. Afternoons—more reports, more emails, credit card charges. The routine only changed on the first of the month when she closed the books.

This morning, as she finished her coffee, something outside caught her eye—a flash of blue in the yard. She set her mug down, wiped the spotless window, and looked closer.

Yes, there was something deep blue, almost purple, in her dirt. Sylvie looked at the clock, retrieved a Post-it note and pen from a small drawer, and wrote: *Check the blue flower.*

She stuck the note to the back door with an extra piece of tape, then got ready for work.

That evening, after putting chicken in the oven, she slipped on her clogs and went outside. To her dismay, the flower was gone. In its place, only a mound of green with a spent bloom. She stared at it for a long moment, then glanced around her yard and went inside.

The next morning, as she ate breakfast standing at the sink, Sylvie nearly dropped her cereal bowl. She forgot to breathe for a moment, frozen, spoon suspended midair as her eyes locked onto the yard.

The flower had returned. And it wasn't alone. A vine curled across the ground, purple blossoms unfurling. Nearby, tiny pink flowers on long stalks waved in the breeze.

She set the bowl down with a clatter, splashed cold water on her face, and checked again. The colors remained. She dashed to the bedroom window—still there.

"What in the world?" she muttered.

Shaken, she wrote another note, though she hardly needed the reminder. She thought of nothing but flowers all day. She even spent lunch researching them—time she usually spent getting ahead on work.

That evening, Sylvie raced home to find the blue flower, once again, had closed for the day, but the others remained, waving at her in the evening breeze. She spent a long time standing among them, turning in quiet circles. As she returned to the house, she spied a single footprint in the soil beneath the vine. Her breath caught. Was it her footprint? She examined it, decided it had to be hers, and went inside to finish her Friday routine.

On an uncharacteristic whim that night, Sylvie grabbed a stepstool and pulled a small box from the top shelf of her storage closet. She opened the box and looked at her old sketchbook and half-used drawing pencils.

"What are you going to do, draw the flowers?" she asked out loud. "Maybe? Tomorrow?"

Stop being frivolous, she thought, echoing the words her mother had said to her thousands of times. She covered the box but left it sitting on the edge of her desk.

The following morning Sylvie peeked out her bedroom window. The entire backyard was covered in plants and blooms—blue spiderworts, purple passion vines, pink paintbrush, yellow daisies. A row of beauty-berry with bright-purple berries lined the back fence.

Unable to contain her excitement, Sylvie stepped outside. She traced each plant and memorized the look of the flowers. Morning light dappled the ground, and even the air seemed brighter, clearer. She wound her way through the plants until she had seen every inch of the yard, committing it all to memory. When she had eyed her fill of the flowers, she turned back to the house. A white square under one of the pine trees caught her eye.

The pocket sketchbook leaned against the tree as if left there by someone who would return any minute. Sylvie looked around the yard; she was, indeed, alone. She bent to retrieve the sketchbook and opened it. Dozens of drawings greeted her, each in her unique whimsical style. And in the corner of each page, a signature remarkably similar to her own—more looped, more artistic—still just one word: *Sylvie*. Impossible! She fled indoors.

That night, she crouched in the dark at the kitchen window, waiting for her midnight gardener to return. When the shadowy figure stepped into view, Sylvie dashed out the back door, flashlight in hand, and beamed the light at the stranger with a timid, "Stop right there!" She stumbled back, heart pounding, the edges of her vision darkening before the world spun away.

When Sylvie came to, she found herself looking into the face of … well, herself. Her oval face, dark hair, hazel eyes, crooked nose from breaking it when she was nine. Fewer lines, happier looking, a glow in that face, but still *her* face.

"You're . . . you're me!" she stammered, scooting backwards away from the stranger-not-stranger.

Her other self smiled, a warmth in her eyes that Sylvie hadn't seen in her own reflection for years. "I'm the you who never stopped dreaming."

"This is insane," Sylvie whispered, clutching the ground for stability. "You can't be real."

"I'm as real as the flowers," her other self said, gesturing to the vibrant garden. "You used to love this—the colors, the freedom. What happened to that girl?"

Sylvie shook her head. "That was a pipe dream. That girl grew up. Frivolous dreams don't pay the bills."

Her other self reached out, brushing a hand over a blooming passion vine. "You sound so much like Mom." A gentle smile touched her face. "It wasn't a pipe dream. In another timeline, I'm—we're—an artist, a pretty darned good one." She reached for Sylvie's hand.

Sylvie shrank against the wall of the house. "No. No! Whatever's going on here, stop it. Just stop! Don't come back, or I'm calling the police." She rushed back indoors. She needed to think. There had to be a sensible, sane, orderly explanation for all of this.

She sat at her desk, ready to find an answer online, but her old sketchbook loomed in the box. She traced a finger over the cover, then closed her eyes. Order. Predictability. Sleep. That's what she needed.

The next morning she found even more plants blooming, dancing in the morning breeze. A smile touched her face, unbidden. It was everything a younger Sylvie had wanted, but this wasn't her dream anymore. She couldn't maintain this natural beauty. All of that gardening took time from her predictable, orderly schedule. And the drawing. She scoffed at the thought. *Frivolous.* That was a long-dead dream.

Wasn't it?

That night, she waited again for her other self, but no one appeared. She sat in the moonlight and watched it play over the flowers, shadows dancing across the ground, the flowers reflecting different shades, and felt a sense of serenity and comfort come over her. She hoped the flowers would still be there in the morning, even if her midnight gardener didn't show.

Sylvie woke Monday morning to a property still filled with the flowers she had grown to love. She sipped her tea and watched butterflies flit among the colors adding to their palette. Then she did something she had never done before—she called in sick. For the first time in years, she felt something stir inside her—a longing she had buried long ago.

She gathered her sketchbook and pencils, poured herself another cup of tea, and ventured outdoors. She sat among the flowers, their colors shifting in the morning light, bees and butterflies weaving past her. Slowly, hesitantly, she began to sketch—the curve of a petal, the arch of a vine, the way the light danced across the leaves.

As the pencil moved across the page, Sylvie felt something she hadn't felt in years—hope. The garden had bloomed and so, perhaps, could she.

The Bridge

by Jim R. Garrison

It was late and dark on the dirt road when two deputies approached the house just outside of Hagerstown, Maryland. The small wood-framed house shared the road with several other similar houses. There weren't any sounds coming from inside the open front door.

Deputy John Hendricks knocked on the door and announced himself. "Clarke County Sheriff's Office. We're coming in."

There was no response.

The deputies drew their side-arms and entered. A man sat slouched on the couch, holding a bottle of whiskey. Blood stained his shirt and a gash ran across his forehead.

"Are you Samuel Reynolds?" John asked.

The man didn't reply. John scanned the room. There were overturned chairs, and a floor lamp lay against the far wall, the light blinking. An iron skillet with blood on it lay on the floor.

His partner, Deputy Ryan Adams, inspected the room. "There's blood over here," he said. "A lot of blood."

"Is there anyone else in the house?" John asked. "Where is your wife?"

Reynolds opened his eyes and just stared at the deputy.

"The caller said they heard screams and a baby crying. I'll ask you again, sir. Where are your wife and child?"

"I don't know." Reynolds took a long swallow, then leaned back and closed his eyes.

John confronted Reynolds again. "What happened here? What did you do?"

Reynolds swiped his forehead and looked at his hand. "The bitch hit me with that." He pointed to the iron skillet on the floor. "The brat wouldn't shut up. That kid cries all the damn time. I made it stop crying."

Ryan knelt where he found the blood. "You better look at this, John."

"Stay where you are," John said, joining his partner. The unmistakable stench of fresh blood on the floor and wall hung in the air, and something or someone had hit the wall hard enough to make an impression in the drywall.

John confronted Reynolds again, "What happened here? What did you do?"

The man lifted the bottle for another swallow, but John slapped it from his hand.

"Talk to me."

"How should I know? The bitch knocked me out with that frying pan."

A woman's voice came from the open doorway. "I saw Nell walking down the road. She was carrying something. I think it might be the baby."

"And you are?" John asked.

"Mary Gerard. I live next door. I'm the one who called." She pointed. "That man there is no good. He's a drunk, and he beats Nell and God knows what else he does. I was afraid for the baby."

John grabbed Reynolds by the arm, yanking him to his feet. "What did you do?" he demanded.

"I didn't do nothin' they don't deserve."

"Cuff him, Ryan, and put him in the cruiser, then call for back-up and CSI. They need to process the scene." He turned to Mary. "Where did you see her?"

"Nell was walking toward the old bridge that goes over the Shenandoah River. I think she was carrying Annie."

"The baby?"

"Yes, that child is only four months old. I hear her crying a lot, and I hear him hollering at them and cursing and banging about." She pointed at Reynolds. "He beats Nell; I've seen her bruises. And I worry for the baby." She looked around the room and saw the blood on the wall. She put her hand to her mouth. "Oh, God! He did something to them, didn't he?"

"Show us where you saw Nell."

Mary pointed. The dirt road was dark and disappeared in that direction. "This road goes across the old river bridge just down the road. She was going that way."

John backed out and sped down the road. Skidding to a stop on the loose gravel just before the bridge, they jumped out of the cruiser.

The full moon cast a silvery light on the bridge and the solitary figure on it. Nell was on the outside of the railing close to the center, holding a bundle clutched to her chest.

The river was black, silent, and waiting. Nell was still as if entranced. Holding the bundle close, she stared into the dark water below.

"Stop!" John called to her. "Don't do it, Nell."

She didn't respond.

As they approached, they heard her speak in a low, strained voice. "Please forgive me, Lord."

Nell leaned out over the dark river with the tiny bundle.

"Nell—Stop," John called to her. "We know what happened. Don't do this."

"I have to," she said with a broken voice. "He killed her."

The detectives moved closer. "We know what he did, Nell. Let us help you."

She shook her head. She was teetering on the wood planks of the bridge, the bundle held precariously in front of her. "It's too late. I let it happen. It's all my fault."

"It's not your fault, Nell. Please don't do this," Ryan pleaded.

Nell stepped forward, but John caught her. She fought to shake him off, but he held tight.

"Let me go, let me go. I have to be with her."

John held on. "I can't let you do this. You have to tell the authorities what he did."

"It doesn't matter anymore. He killed Annie, and I let it happen."

Ryan pried the bundle from Nell, and John wrapped his arms around her. "It's not your fault, Nell."

"Your husband will answer for what he's done." John helped her off the bridge with Ryan following with the bloody bundle.

When Nell saw her husband in the back of the cruiser, she froze. "What is he doing here?"

"He's being arrested and going to jail. Is there someplace where you can stay?"

Mary arrived after a fast walk. She overheard John's question and, breathing hard, she said, "Nell can stay at our house." She took Nell from John and wrapped her arms around her. "Where's Annie, Nell?"

Nell looked back at Ryan who still held the bundle.

Mary let out a sigh of relief, "Thank God."

Nell was shaking her head. "He killed her, Mary."

Mary looked at the two deputies. They nodded. The bundle Ryan held was covered in blood.

Reynolds yelled from the back seat of the cruiser, "Tell them, Nell. Tell them what you did."

Nell stared at him. "What *I* did? *You* threw Annie against that wall. *You* broke her, Sam."

He shook his head wildly. "You lying bitch. You're the one who did it. You killed our baby and then you tried to kill me with that frying pan."

John said, "We'll see what the district attorney has to say."

Several minutes later, the CSI team, another sheriff's cruiser, and EMS personnel arrived. A uniformed man and woman exited the ambulance and carefully accepted the bundle from Ryan. The deputy's words caught in his throat as he explained, "The baby is dead. Her head was smashed."

John looked at Sam in the back of the cruiser and said under his breath to Ryan, "She should have hit that man harder."

Mary told Nell, "Let's go to my house and let these people do their job."

"That's a good idea," John said. "The detectives will meet with you and Nell shortly."

Nell shook her head. "No, I can't leave Annie."

Mary hugged her. "Annie's gone to another dimension, Nell. She's in Heaven with God and all the angels. Nothing can ever hurt her again."

When Nell's tears finally came, her body trembled with sobs that came from deep inside her. Her eyes flooded with tears that ran down her cheeks as she watched them carry the small bundle to the ambulance.

Getting Aweigh

by Lorrie Gault

Margo needed breathing space. Frustration had dug in deep, and punching pillows did little to ease her boyfriend troubles.

"Kevin is driving me ca-*razy*," she vented to her pal, Gabby, after their morning jog.

Gabby bent over, attempting to catch her breath in the Phoenix heat. "Have you tried reasoning with him?"

"Yup. Not working. Last night, last straw." She fanned herself with her wide-brimmed hat. "I stood on a stepstool in my four-inch heels so we could go nose-to-nose and told him to take a long walk off a short pier. Delivered with snarky overtones. Nasty, even."

"You are a firecracker. And then?"

"He thought I was joking." She shook her head and tucked a sweaty strand of copper hair behind her ear.

"You *were* joking, right?"

"Sometimes I feel like I'm being guarded by a 280-pound rottweiler. He hovers, Gabs, and glares at people. I'm suffocating." She kicked at a few pebbles. "You're my all-knowing best friend. I need a solution and I'm not coming up with one. Help, please."

Gabby patted her on the shoulder. "Okay, my opinion? I admit my brother can be a bit clingy and overprotective. Why? Because you're tiny and because he's an NFL tackle who acts like one. Look, it's off-season. Be happy he prefers you to his hulk buddies." She took a long drink from her water bottle, giving her point time to sink in. "Honestly, Margo, you're overreacting. Kevin's a teddy bear. He *loves* you. Everybody can see that." She peered at Margo over the top of her glasses, then huffed when Margo's response was a death stare. "Nevertheless, as you said, we *are* besties. So let me give it a think."

Margo clasped her hands together and bowed. "Bless you, my savior."

A week later, Gabby, clutching a folder, slid into a diner booth across from Margo.

"What's that?"

"You wanted a solution." Gabby shrugged. "This one is far-fetched, but it's all I've got since you're in such a hurry."

"And it is . . .?"

"Remember my cousin, the Cirque du Soleil juggler reject? He got a gig on a cruise ship and said they have more short-term positions available. I'm not wild about the idea, but check out this list anyway. Mind you, though, they're not looking for math teachers."

Margo grabbed the folder. After a quick perusal of its contents, she shouted, "This! This one here." She spun the folder around for Gabby to read and pointed to a line halfway down the page. "It's over summer break. Good thing I've had that part-time casino gig since grad school. I'm telling you, it's perfect."

Gabby took a peek and sat back in her chair. "You're serious?"

Margo nodded like a bobblehead.

"Okay," Gabby said after a beat. "Maybe you need a change more than I thought. Go find your Zen, honey. Just remember, you're used to being landlocked in the Arizona desert."

Yes, it'll be a whole new world totally away from Kevin. Margo wiggled her eyebrows and beamed.

She sailed through her Zoom interview, securing the job without a hitch. Three weeks later, after a cool goodbye to Kevin, she flew to Florida and rolled her luggage onto the ship at the Port of Miami. Although the "boat," as she called it, was much smaller than she had imagined, she still tingled with anticipation at beginning her new position as a blackjack dealer.

"A three-month contract won't bother me," she'd told Gabby. "It'll give me time to think. I'll be snug as a bug in my cabin and unreachable by Kevin. Plus, I love the whole gambling vibe. Best of all worlds, babe."

It didn't take long for her enthusiasm to flag. An unknown predisposition for seasickness revealed itself soon after the ship set sail. Twelve miles from shore, with the wind kicking up and the ocean choppy, Margo's roiling stomach emptied its contents on the fine felt fabric of her assigned blackjack table. If embarrassment had been a python, it would have swallowed her whole.

She apologized and galloped hot-faced to sick bay where the doc slapped a motion sickness patch behind her ear. "Perhaps this isn't the job for you," he said not unkindly. *Little late for that*, Margo thought.

On a slow-march back to the casino, she was intercepted by her surly manager who led her straight to a table in the smoking section. "Penance," he said before clamping a handkerchief to his nose and scurrying away. Six impatient players puffed on cigars that enveloped Margo in a pungent, smoky haze. *I can do this*, she thought, and by taking miniscule breaths remained stoic for the next two hours.

About to pat herself on the back for persevering, she was instead derailed again, this time by a loudmouthed, drunken gambler. As he strolled around the tables with a demure younger woman, he blathered on about heading for the Bermuda Triangle. *Whaaat?* Why hadn't she bothered to focus on the itinerary? Was flight from Kevin worth possible death by unknown phenomena? Cold sweat surfaced on her upper lip. Her head pounded as Lady Gaga belted out "rain on me, tsu-na-mi" in the background. The ship seemed to rock and roll even more with the music. She gulped. *Oh, terrific. We're all gonna die.*

She pinched herself and tried to focus. When a player yelled "hit me" three times before she dealt him a card, she begged the dealer on break to relieve her for a quick sec, ignoring his eye roll. She ducked into an alcove, leaned against a wall, and prayed not to have a panic attack. *Deep breaths, Margo.*

"You all right, darlin'?" a smarmy passenger asked her, sidling up way too close. "I got a nice bottle of champagne chillin' in my suite," he whispered and licked his cracked lips. The ick factor made Margo want to crawl into a deep, hot bubble bath. She longed to dig her spike heel into his sandaled foot but couldn't afford to make more waves. Who wanted a whiny woman assaulting the casino patrons her first day on the job? Who would fend off the vermin on her behalf? Kevin flickered across her mind before she gritted her teeth, brushed past the creepy guy, and hurried back to her table.

Still nauseous and shaking like an aspen leaf at midnight, a final indignity befell her after the theft of several high-value chips from her table. The first one accused? New girl. Security personnel detained Margo in a locked room while they sifted through footage from their omnipresent cameras, roundly ignoring her repeated, fervent denials until they identified and apprehended the real thief at 3:00 a.m.—the unassuming female accomplice of the loudmouthed drunk.

Margo had had enough. She countered security's lukewarm apologies with a demand: cancel her contract and allow her to disembark at the first port of call or expect to be notified by her attorney. The cruise line honchos agreed without argument, in fact, encouraged it.

Margo flew back to Phoenix annoyed with herself, but mostly introspective. She thought hard about her impulsivity and its effect on her life choices. Perhaps she had been a bit hasty with her decisions. Clearly, she was not cut out for the world of cruise ship travel on large bodies of unpredictable water. *What's most important to you, Margo?* she asked herself many times. *What do you really want?*

When she saw Kevin's eager face at the gate, everything crystalized.

"Hi, Boo," he said. "Welcome back. I've missed you." He placed a tentative hand on her cheek. "Sis said you'd come around. Is that true? I just had to be patient . . . and rethink my guard-dog habits."

Margo smiled. "I did say Gabby was all-knowing."

On impulse, she laid her carry-on suitcase in front of him. Although not quite as tall or sturdy as her stepstool, she balanced on top of it in her four-inch heels and faced him *almost* nose-to-nose.

"I'm sorry, Kevey," she said. "There's no place like home and no one better to come home to."

He wrapped his strong, protective arms around her. This felt brand new and wonderful. She didn't mind it one bit.

Synchronicity

by Bill Griffith

Agentle ache in Ben's jaw reminded him that smiling for an extended amount of time results in the muscles in one's jaw developing fatigue. Allowing his head to flop back on the seat of the school bus, he closed his eyes. The face and voice of the tour guide illuminated in his mind.

"General Longstreet was General Sumner's best man at Sumner's wedding. But at Antietam these best friends found themselves on opposite sides of a futile battle. They drove their armies into a blood bath of horrendous proportions and in the end neither man would claim victory."

September meant football season, less humidity and relief from the summer heat. Ben loved everything about football—the thrill of the competition and even the workouts were cool, but his passion on this day was reliving those moments from the deadliest single day of the Civil War. His fingers clenched as he imagined the two massive armies colliding on that fateful day in September of 1862. He wondered if the soldiers noticed the beauty of the forests that surrounded the farmland of Antietam. His mind answered, *how could they appreciate anything in the chaos that ensued? A horror that took thirty-two men every minute for twelve hours.*

"Bedtime big man." Ben's father's voice had that familiar bass drum effect as it echoed up the stairs.

Closing his math book, Ben thought his father would make a wonderful drill sergeant. Before shutting off the light next to his bed, he studied the posters on his ceiling that portrayed a myriad of constellations. Each star reminded him of the men who fought in waves like army ants. Every soldier had a dream and purpose. But in the end, they were the barter war demands. Statistics in another history book. The highlight of another tour.

Ben traveled in dream space. Fatigue from football practice combined with walking the fields of Antietam caused his mind to float. Something unseen carried him with a gentle current as his soul meandered far away from the real world.

His next conscious thoughts came without warning. The rancid stench from an unnatural fire caused his nostrils to constrict, and he felt his body lunge as he sneezed. In the midst of a deep sleep, he felt his mouth open and close and his tongue work to wipe away the caustic flavor of the air. His skin began to crawl from a slimy airborne debris he did not recognize. His attempts to generate enough saliva to wash away the horrid taste of smoke were futile. Having never witnessed it, somehow, he knew it anyway—the fires had the stench of burning flesh. The sounds of gun fire and screaming men added to his horror. When the curtain rose on his visual senses, he found himself staring down the barrel of a rifle. His body was clothed in a dark-blue uniform, and along with several other men, he was kneeling behind a shoddy barricade constructed of fenceposts, tree trunks, branches, mud, and random stones.

At some distance, soldiers dressed in gray jackets marched up the hill. Confederates—intent on taking the ground Ben and his fellow Union soldiers defended. Thick black and gray smoke from numerous brush fires concealed the progress of the enemy.

"Sir, the Reb's are hiding behind their dead. They're stacking bodies as cover." The words came from a soldier standing next to Ben.

"Make sure you don't waste a shot." Ben heard his own voice and felt his lips move. But his mind made him aware . . . *this is another world.*

Turning his attention to the battlefield, the target was not thirty feet away. His hand fell from the barrel of his gun as he made a futile attempt to block the blinding flash erupting from the barrel of the rifle of the soldier next to him. A Confederate collapsed to his knees and uttered a terrible wail. Blood erupted from his chest. The enemy's proximity made the killing more personal. Ben's rifle shifted to the left and his sights fell on a boy's face. Mud and dirt coated his left cheek. Short and thin, his head didn't reach the shoulders of the men he fought beside. Black hair, slick with sweat, draped down over his ears and onto his neck. The men were looking for cover, but this boy charged forward. Blue eyes and clenched teeth were the portrait of mindless rage. The young man's bayonet sparkled from the flashes of light erupting from the firestorm on either side of Ben. Although it remained a dream, Ben imagined the blade piercing his chest.

When the boy was close enough for Ben to discern three separate colors in his plaid shirt, he pulled the trigger. The rifle bucked, and smoke flooded his senses. When everything cleared, he couldn't believe his eyes. The shot had torn the belt buckle off the young man and his pants had fallen to his boots. He stood in the field staring down at his pants as blood spewed from his stomach. Raising his head, the boy stared at Ben. Lifting his arms, he remained silent as he fell face forward on the ground. In those moments, Ben could not stop looking at the boy's hair. It was more magnificent than the models in his mother's fashion magazines. Perfect hair on a dead boy.

"Hey Bazooka Boy!" A familiar voice rang from behind Ben as he stood at his locker.

Three of his best friends walked up behind him with a fourth boy Ben did not recognize. His face was turned down as his friend Phillip spoke.

"Bazooka Boy is our middle linebacker. He can crunch most any asshole. Trouble is his brains are mush. I'll introduce you, but he may not remember your name tomorrow."

Ben's three friends all laughed, but the stranger kept his head turned down. The boy was short and didn't appear to carry much muscle. But something about him looked familiar.

After punching Ben's shoulder, Phillip continued, "Ben my boy, this is Pete; he just moved into town and, according to Coach, this guy can run like a deer. Sounds like we might have a real free safety when we go up against Brockton in a couple of weeks."

At that point, Pete looked up. Ben swallowed hard and fell back against his locker. The plaid shirt with the same colors and that face. Those blue eyes and his perfect teeth . . . but most of all the black hair that covered his ears and fell gently on his shoulders. Ben stood in front of a living ghost. Pete didn't speak but nodded and offered his hand. Ben stood a good four inches taller than Pete, but his hand was shaking and he found it impossible to lift his arm.

Later that afternoon during history class, Ben's teacher had everyone's attention. "I want you all to think about the most memorable moments from our tour of the Battlefield of Antietam. Take five minutes and jot down your highlights. You'll have a chance to share these with the rest of us."

After listening to many of his friends relate moments of bravery from both sides of the battle, it was finally Ben's turn to speak.

"War offers a license to kill. To this end Antietam was a great success. Men died hiding behind cornstalks. Dust bowls clouded the battlefield which allowed many to die without being noticed. Neither army found victory at Antietam. But death had a wonderful day. Antietam was a farm that became a massive cemetery—a slaughterhouse for men. History is written by the living. I wonder how differently the text books would read if the dead had a voice in the matter."

Serendipity

by Ellen P. Holder

Serendipity: The phenomenon of finding valuable things not sought for.

Traci sat on a park bench in the small town where she'd spent her life. Tears ran down her cheeks, and she wiped them away with bare hands. Her prospects were discouraging, and—just her luck—a man in dirty, worn-out clothes eased down next to her. The area was deserted, and her pulse raced; how could she get help, even if she yelled and screamed?

"What's up, kid? You need a pal?" he said while his eyes roamed over her body.

"No thanks. I want to be alone."

The guy didn't budge. "You ain't gonnna make it on your own. You need somebody to protect you from what you run into at night. People like us do better paired up."

"People like us? I'm not homeless," she sputtered. *Not yet anyway.*

He stood and gave her a creepy smile. "Okay, Miss Priss. You change your mind, ask around for Kurt. Lotta girls know me," he said, reaching to touch her blond hair.

Traci clutched her purse and ran in the opposite direction, racing down the street that took her into the heart of town. She trudged along the sidewalk, wondering how she could keep her job washing dishes at Rosie's Diner. She couldn't dress well enough to be a waitress. Customers couldn't see her in the kitchen but, even there, her faded, thrift-shop clothing should be clean every day.

The thin, pale girl with short hair avoided looking at herself in the store windows; she disliked her appearance and had more important things to think about. She had just graduated from high school, finally able to work full time, but would soon be kicked out of the foster home she'd lived in the past six months . . . simply because she was turning eighteen.

She had no relatives, no close friends, and not nearly enough money saved to pay the deposit on a rental unit. She'd spent years saving money. But no matter where she lived, someone went through her things, and her money always disappeared.

Traci's stomach growled, and she stopped at Rosie's, even though she was not scheduled to work that day. They were past the lunchtime rush, and she found an empty booth. Someone had left their newspaper behind; she could search the classified ads.

Earl came over and asked if she wanted to order anything. "Wish I could," she said. "Can I get a glass of water?"

Earl wasn't much older than Traci. He squinted his eyes at her. "I'll bring you a soda. It's on me."

She wasn't used to kindness and raised her eyebrows. "Thanks! I could use a Coke."

Traci thumbed through the ads and saw nothing priced low enough. Where would she sleep? Where would she keep her few possessions? Where would she bathe and prepare for work each day?

One of the ads caught her eye. Not because she saw a good deal, but because she noticed the sloppy spelling and punctuation. "For *Sale*" was spelled "For *Sell*." And who couldn't spell *Chevrolet*? Maybe it was just a typo when they left out the *r*. But she saw similar typos all over the page.

She needed to get back "home" and help Ms. Jenkins. Ignoring Traci's urgent need to find another home, Ms. Jenkins insisted she had to earn her keep. And every minute Traci was not working at the diner, Ms. Jenkins kept her busy with housework.

Traci looked back at the ads. She'd be walking past the newspaper office on her way home, and she might just show this paper to the manager. She sipped on her Coke and marked the errors with Earl's ballpoint pen.

Ten minutes later, she stood in front of Mr. Wilkins' desk—not just the manager but the owner of *Evansdale News*. Her courage almost forsook her, but she had nothing to lose. "I only need a few minutes of your time," she said. "I'm Traci Smith. I graduated from high school last month, so I haven't been to college. Maybe someday," she added wistfully. "I just want to point out some of these errors. I only looked at the ads, but there are so many mistakes and typos. Does anybody proofread this before printing?"

Mr. Wilkins bunched his lips to one side, looking thoughtful. "Yes, I do have someone. But they're not really suited for this job, I guess." He tapped the paper in all the places she'd circled. "I don't have time to pore over it myself."

He glanced up at Traci and her sharp, intelligent eyes. "You want to show me what you got?"

"Excuse me?" she asked.

"What I mean is how about you take the front page and this red pen, go sit at that empty desk, and mark everything you find wrong. Then I'll know you did the corrections yourself."

"Oh, was I insulting when I brought this in here? I didn't mean it. I'm just upset today, looking for a place to live."

He gave her an odd look. "No offense taken. Just show me some of your work."

Traci reached for the newspaper and pen, then sat at the desk he'd indicated and got to work. At one point, she giggled but clapped her hand over her mouth. When she heard, "Ten minutes. Time's up," she rose and carried the paper back to him.

Mr. Wilkins took the paper. Seeing all the red marks, he raised his eyebrows. Seconds later, he roared with laughter. He reached for his handkerchief and wiped his eyes.

"You wouldn't think people still had outdoor toilets in their backyards," he said. "And I wouldn't have thought our proofreader would miss this typo." The front-page article was titled, City Ordinance Demands Removal of Outdoor Toilets. A photo was included, with a caption which should have read: *One of several shots taken around town.*

But, in "shots" there was a typo. Whoever typed the caption had hit the *i* instead of the *o*.

They laughed together, and he turned his attention back to her corrections. "Young lady, it looks like I need you working for me."

Traci held onto the front of his desk so she wouldn't fall over. "Me?" she said. "Sir, are you serious?"

"Absolutely. You'd have to fill out an application, but just as a formality. I like your spunk and honesty almost as much as I value your skill."

I have spunk? And skill? "Sir, there is a problem. In two weeks, I'll be eighteen, and I'll be evicted from my foster home. I have no idea where I'll live." She felt her face heat up. "I might be homeless."

"Come with me," he said, rising from his seat. He led her through other offices to the back of the building and to a small room with outside access. It had a window, a sturdy cot, and a bathroom. "Will this do?"

Traci's eyes filled with tears. To her, it looked like a peaceful hideaway. "I would be so grateful. But who's using it now?"

Mr. Wilkins blushed. "It's where I sometimes take a nap when I eat a heavy lunch. You can have it till you find a better place, and I'll give you the only key."

Back in the front office, Mr. Wilkins handed Traci the application. "Take it home and fill it out, then bring it back tomorrow." He gestured to the back offices. "You'll only have a cubicle, but you can make it your own." His face turned solemn. "I'll expect good work. You won't let me down, will you?"

"Never!" she promised.

She shook Mr. Wilkins's hand and left the office with her head up and her shoulders straight, trembling with excitement. She was *skilled*, she was *valued*.

With every step, she saw a future with endless possibilities, and her world felt like a whole new universe.

Your Turn

by Henry James Kaye

The old man, Haadi, sat at his regular table in the park by himself, shoulders slumped, hands clasped in his lap, head down. To the casual observer, he looked asleep. His faded, long-sleeved shirt looked several sizes too big. The half-glasses perched on his nose's end needed a good cleaning.

When a thin boy, wearing a tattered T-shirt, about age fourteen, plopped onto the chair across from him, Haadi opened his eyes and took in the red-faced, panting boy who twisted to look in the opposite direction.

Slowly and deliberately, the man reached to the chessboard before him with an arthritic hand and moved a white pawn. In a scratchy voice he mumbled, "Your turn."

"Wait. What?" the boy stammered. He turned to the old man and then the direction he'd come from. He stiffened, then turned to face the board, pretending he had become engrossed in playing chess.

A winded, overweight man lumbered to the table and shook a fist at the boy. "You stole candy bars, you thief. Don't move. I'll have you arrested."

Haadi raised a hand and looked at the man. "Sir, you are interrupting our contest. Please leave us alone so we can play in peace."

The young boy nodded, turned his attention to the chess board, and moved a black pawn.

The heavy man waved his arms, pointed a pudgy index finger at the boy, and sputtered, "All right, I'll let you go this time, but don't ever come to my shop again, or you'll regret it." He stomped away a couple of steps, then bellowed, "I'm warning you, don't come back."

Before the boy could respond, Haadi raised his hand and moved a white bishop. "Your turn."

The boy had rudimentary chess knowledge from school and, unsure what to do next, moved another black pawn forward.

Haadi grimaced and looked over the top of his half-glasses. "I see you haven't played much chess." He moved his white queen diagonally, several rows. "Your turn."

"Hey, old man, I know what I'm doing. You just watch your step." The boy studied the board briefly, tapping a finger against his cheek. "Hmmm. I have a lot of options. Which one do I choose?" He extracted three ChocoHunk candy bars from a pants pocket, opened one, and ate half of it in one bite. After looking at the board for a few more seconds, he shrugged and moved another pawn forward. He leaned back and folded his arms across his chest. "Your turn," he said with a smile, shoving the remaining candy bar piece in his mouth.

"Yes, it is my turn." Without hesitation, Haadi moved his queen forward and captured a black pawn. "Checkmate."

The boy leaned forward, forehead wrinkled. "But . . . how did you do that so fast?"

"I put my efforts into studying the game, not stealing candy bars." He rested his hands in his lap. "Think about what you did. Come back tomorrow without being chased, and I'll teach you. Now leave."

"But . . . that must be some trick. I'll be back tomorrow." The boy stood. "You won't trick me again. No sir, I'll beat you tomorrow."

Haadi's eyebrows rose. "I will see you tomorrow. Now go." He lowered his head and closed his eyes.

The next day, the boy arrived at the park mid-morning, sat at Haadi's table, and boldly stated, "I figured out what you did. You won't fool me again." He boldly moved a pawn forward one space. "There. How's that grab you?"

"Good block. I see you have learned. What is your name?"

He paused for a few seconds, seemingly unsure whether to be honest or not, shrugged, and responded, "Randall."

"Randall, here is your next lesson." Within two minutes, Haadi checkmated the kid.

Randall stood, replayed the moves aloud, and grumbled.

"Go, study more. I will see you tomorrow and use a new gambit. Be prepared."

Randall scratched his head. "What's a gambit?"

Haadi studied Randall's face before answering. "It's an opening in which a player, me, obtains an advantage by sacrificing a piece to you."

"I don't get it. Why would you do that?"

"You will learn tomorrow. Now go."

The daily lessons continued throughout the summer. Each day, Randall sat across from Haadi, confidently moving his pieces until he realized he'd been outmaneuvered. He couldn't get ahead of the old man despite studying chess moves for hours every afternoon and evening.

One day, at the end of summer, almost an hour into a match, Randall straightened, studied the board and then tipped over his king. "I surrender. By the way, I won't be here the next few days, I . . ."

Haadi raised a hand. For the first time, Randall noticed how thin the crooked fingers had become, and the skin seemed translucent. Haadi looked tired.

"No need to talk. You have learned well, and I have reached the end of my ability to teach you. Now go."

"I'll be back Saturday."

"Do as you wish." He closed his eyes, lowered shaking hands into his lap, and hung his head.

While walking across the park, Randall reflected on the brief conversation. *The old man didn't say, "I'll see you Saturday." Why not? He always said I'll see you . . .*

Saturday morning, with the sun shining, birds chirping, and a spring in his step, Randall crossed the park to what he'd come to think of as The Old Man's Table.

To his surprise, an old woman sat at the table with Haadi's chess set in front of her. She sat on the black side, the side Randall always sat on. The white side, Haadi's, was open. Randall approached the table and noticed the woman sat like the old man: slumped shoulders, hands in her lap, head down. When he neared the table, she looked at him through sad eyes.

"Hi, I normally play with the old man that plays chess here. Do you know if he's here?" Randall looked around to see if he was at a different table.

Her eyes filled with tears, and she extended her hand. Randall took the soft hand and shook it once.

"Haadi is my husband. He sent me here to give you his chess set."

Randall stiffened and let go of her hand like he'd touched a hot stove. "No. It's his. I don't want it."

"Sweetheart, he has no use for it any longer and wanted you to have it."

"I'll pay him for it. Where is he?" Randall licked his lips and looked around with wide eyes.

"He won't be coming any longer." Her eyes grew even sadder.

Randall gasped, and his hand flew to his mouth. "No. It can't be. He didn't . . ."

She nodded. "He is gone. Three days ago." A tear trickled down each cheek.

"Oh my God." He reached out and rested his hand on the table to steady himself. "No, it can't be."

"Please. Sit." She pointed to the empty chair. "I have something to share with you."

"I . . . I can't sit there. That's his seat." He shook his head.

"It is your chair now. One of the last things he told me was that you were his best student. This is your chess set now. You earned it."

Randall wiped tears from his cheeks. "I . . . I don't know what to say. I knew he was old, but I didn't know he was . . . sick."

"At the beginning of summer, they told him he had two weeks. He came here that day wanting one last game. He met you and then insisted he needed to come here to teach you. You needed a new direction, and he wanted to help you discover it."

"I found it. I learned to study. I'm happy to be back in school. All because of the old man."

"His name is Haadi. H-A-A-D-I. In our language, it means guide or leader. He said he'd never been a guide, but when he met you, he believed he could accomplish the name his parents blessed him with. You made them proud." She rose, looked him in the eye, and smiled. "Thank you."

Tears trickled down his cheeks as he watched her shuffle away.

"Cool. Chess," a new voice said.

He turned and saw a kid, about twelve, ChocoHunk candy bar in hand, seated in his old chair.

"Can you teach me?" the kid asked.

Randall wiped his cheeks and sat. He moved a white pawn. "Your turn."

Beyond the Gates

by KE Manning

"We shouldn't be down here. Someone's going to find us."

Light peeked down between the floorboards, casting lines of brightness onto the two young women crammed beneath the old house.

Lara gave the person beside her a firm, if not squinted, look. "No one will find us, Mary, so long as you keep your mouth shut. Now hush." She turned back to peering up between the dusty boards, trying to catch sight of the two men who shared the small room above.

Warren moved into sight, sallow-cheeked and red-eyed, arms crossed over a faded shirt and badge. He always tried his best to fill out the sagging blue uniform of the man who had worn it last.

"I'm sorry, Mal, but this was decided the day you came to us." He inclined his head toward where the other man stood—or leaned, rather. Lara knew he would be leaning, as if standing straight was something that did not come naturally to him. "It's just not in the best interest of the town."

The floorboards creaked with the shifting of a man's weight upon them.

"This town has a future because of what I do beyond those gates."

Mal's voice was rough, measured, and Lara's pulse quickened with each word. It brought her back to the moment they'd met, when she'd been just a girl with mud on her knees and knots in her hair. The day the gates opened.

She remembered the creaking of the hinges, rusted and sticky from disuse, rising above the angry voices protesting the admittance of the strangers from the outside.

That was the first time she had seen him—a small figure hooded and clad in filth, clutching the hand of a woman who looked unsteady on her feet. The pair had advanced determinedly forward as if on a mission, and Lara doubted that had the doors remained closed it would have held them back for long.

The Nothingness, the desolation that whistled and burned at their backs, made her clutch her weather-beaten doll close until the doors closed again. People didn't come from the Nothingness. People were sent out, but no one returned. The gates never opened.

The woman collapsed upon entrance. When her knees hit the ground, the figure beside her pulled back his hood and screamed for help. That was the first time she saw Mal, a boy with his face creased with soot and eyes like burning candles in the dark.

She'd never seen eyes like that before—blue, clouded over to milky white. Back then, it had scared her. Now, it was normal; it was Mal, and she loved those eyes more than any other.

Warren cleared his throat, adjusting his stance, placing gnarled hands onto his cracked leather belt. "You're an outsider. This town might have taken you and your mother in, but don't believe for a second you're one of us."

There was a long pause where Lara could do nothing but stare at the uncomfortable face of their newly appointed sheriff.

"I believe I've more than paid my dues to this town," Mal said. "Enough to be considered a part of it."

"And you are. Everyone appreciates what you do and the risks you take. But what people love you for, they fear you for. No one leaves these walls, no one except you. And you keep coming back alive." Warren sighed. "You bring good bounty back more times than not, and we've never asked how. But people don't trust what they don't understand. I'm sorry, but Lara is destined for another. It's already been decided. There's got to be an order to things. How come you never told anyone how you and your mother arrived at our doorstep?"

There was another long pause. "It's nobody's business but ours."

"Uh-huh." Warren shook his head. "No one knows what you were exposed to or where you came from. It doesn't look good. Not for us or Lara."

"So I'm good enough to risk my life, but not good enough to marry one of your women? I'm just a workhorse that stumbled into your fields?"

Warren exhaled loudly. "You know as well as I do it's more than that. Your eyes have the milk in them. People know what that means. It wouldn't be fair to us or Lara if I approved a marriage like that. The population needs to grow, Mal. We can't die off."

Lara felt a weight pressing down on her chest. She'd heard what people said about cloudy eyes.

"He's infertile," Mary whispered.

"Hush," Lara snapped.

"And it's not just that," Warren continued. "We've other problems. Population problems."

"Population? You just said—"

"I'm talking about the male population. Too many men, not enough women." Warren shifted uncomfortably. "There's been talk of sharing."

Mal lowered his voice. "Sharing?"

Warren shrugged. "It's important we keep up morale. For the good of the town."

"Whose morale?" Mal asked, his words full of gravel and darkness.

"What's he saying?" Mary asked, voice small and numb.

"That we're nothing but cattle." Lara swallowed back the dread that had so quickly replaced her hope. "You heard the sheriff. Got to keep up morale."

"Can't you two just be happy being friends?" Warren asked.

"I don't believe we can." Mal stepped into view, boots and long coat mere inches from Lara's touch. "What you're saying. It's not right and you know it."

"It's survival, Mal."

"It's cruel."

Silence enveloped the room. Warren chewed his lip. "If you can't accept it, maybe it's time you moved on."

"Might be."

Fabric fluttered. Footsteps creaked across the boards, showering dust onto Lara and Mary. A door opened and shut. Boots crunched outside.

"Do you think it's true?" Mary whispered frantically. "Do we even get a say?"

Lara looked over—her head pounding. Mary looked just as she felt—scared.

"That's not going to be me," Lara said, inching her way out from beneath the house.

The light of the remaining day fell upon Lara's head as she crawled into the open, Mary close behind. The haze in the air made her guess the sun was about to set.

"Lara."

They whipped around. Mal leaned against the back of the house, waiting. His hat was pulled low over his eyes, his beard tangled. He straightened as she approached.

"You knew I'd be listening?" she asked.

He nodded. "I know you well enough."

"They can't do this. What Warren said . . . it's slavery."

"They can." Mal pushed a strand of hair behind her ear. "Warren's right. I can't give you children."

"I don't care about that." Lara grabbed his lapels, pulling him closer. "I won't let them use me. I'd rather die."

"Lara," Mary cautioned.

"What does it matter?" Lara looked at the makeshift buildings pieced together with scraps and odds and ends. People milled along the dusty paths. She had no surviving family. Mal was all she had.

She turned back to him. "We can leave this place. Be together—"

"What do you mean leave? Where else would you . . ." Mary's voice drifted off. "You can't," she whispered. "It's suicide."

Mal touched Lara's hands, squeezing lightly. "You don't know what that means."

"I lost my sister at fourteen. My parents lived to thirty-five. I'm eighteen now, if I've kept my months straight." She squeezed his hands tighter. "I would rather die with you out there than live without you here."

Mal stared at her with his milky blue eyes; his cracked hat pushed back against a forehead lined with sweat and worry. Then, he smiled.

"Mary," he said. "Tell them to open the gates. We're on our way out."

Lara returned his smile. Despite the fear of the Nothingness beyond the walls, she felt happy. She felt right. He was all she had left.

Bugs 'n' Bubba

by Chris Marek

A campfire warms my denim jacket. A canopy of stars forms delicate theater lighting for the rustic stage that is my campsite. Trees stand like ushers waiting for a show to begin.

Policy meetings? Quarterly reports? I can no longer tell if that world I left behind is even real. And this mountain air! May it work its magic this evening.

I reach into my cooler, pull out a beer, and release my mind to the mesmerizing fire . . .

From the woods' edge near my campsite, out of night's mysterious murk, a form emerges. Feet press dry leaves, yet I hear no sound. Legs brush wispy weeds that do not bend. In a mere blink of time, the form arrives at the edge of my campsite, and from the background of shadows and dim outlines, materializes a young man in jeans, flannel shirt, and a ball cap—his face aglow in campfire light. I am sure I have never seen him, yet he has the friendly manner of a familiar.

He smiles and says, "Evenin'. I'm Bugs. How ya doin'?"

"Fine. Won't you join me?"

"Thanks."

He sits. I offer him a beer from the cooler between our chairs, and we settle back. Bugs pops open a beer while my can remains unopened. I sense he has something on his mind, so I wait. He glances toward the woods—and whatever world he came from—then looks into the fire.

"So, back in the Ozarks," he begins, "I lived way down in the holler. Had this ol' pickup truck passed down to me—fixed up nice. It drove in a straight line and, like the better trucks in those parts, it had working brakes."

The better trucks? Working brakes? Okay.

"So, it's real cold. Rainin'. I get this truck to climb up outta that holler and onto the road, ol' Highway-23, headin' out to my job. Then I get to some tight curves. Pop-Tart I was eatin' falls un'erneath the seat. I reach down to pick it up. I look back up and now I'm seein' nothin' but woods through the windshield. I overcorrect, and when I do, it's wet; I had bald tires 'cause I had no money for good tires." Bugs waves his beer can in the firelight. "I go slippin' and slidin' like I usually do, but this time that truck rolls right off into the ditch."

He takes another swig, his eyes brightening with remembrance.

"Truck winds up on its left side and, of course, I wasn't wearin' my seatbelt, so I had hit my head on the windshield, busted it up, and now I'm bleedin' a bit."

He hits the windshield with his head, and it's the glass *that breaks?*

"So, I climb out, and I'm sittin' on top of the truck on the passenger side door cuz this thing's on its side now. Buddy, I know if I can't get this fixed, I'll have to hoof it back home."

Bugs sets down an empty beer can and reaches into the cooler for another.

"Now keep in mind, I can't afford no tow truck, so I gotta figure this out the ol' back roads way, right?"

I could only wonder what way that was.

"So, 'long comes a guy in a ol' pickup truck who lives in those parts. We call him Bubba. His real name is Bartholomew, but ever'one calls him Bubba."

I nod as if I am used to such names.

"So Bubba stops and says, 'Hey, man! 'Ya need some help?'"

"I say, 'Buddy, ya got that right.'"

"He says, Ah'll get out muh chains. We'll get ya turned out right and see if this thing'll go.'"

"But then Bubba steps a little closer. He asks, 'Have you called the pohlice?'"

I wonder if it's time to pop open my beer.

Bugs continued. "Now, Bubba's not a bad guy. He's just one of these country boys, and he was a lot like his daddy, who was never quite on the right side of the law."

"What happened to him?"

"Pohlice came to serve him papers. He met 'em on the front porch with a shotgun. Shot him ninety-seven times."

The first ninety-six bullets weren't enough?

Bugs slams back more beer. "So, Bubba lived in a shack deep in those woods. Hardly ever worked more than three days at a time in his life. I never knew how he made his money—no one knew exactly—but it sure weren't legal. He ain't a bad guy, though."

"By 'shack,' do you mean a house?"

"Yeah, a shack-house." Bugs crinkles an empty can in one hand and pulls out the next one. "Built it himself. Been workin' on it since high school. Some day it'll even have a front door—hinges an' everythin'."

Yes, hinges and front doors are nice. The fire has lost some of its warmth, and I add some firewood.

"So, we get my truck flipped back up using some ol' country tricks, and by now some folks are startin' to pull over and take pictures with their phone cameras. Bubba hisses, 'Bet one o' them city folks called the pohlice!'"

"I say, 'Prolly not, good buddy. Let's get this truck goin'.'"

"Getting louder now, Bubba says 'I ain't got no insurance! I ain't got no registration! I gotta warrant in Ozark County. I AIN'T GONNA LET 'EM GET ME!'" Then he turns toward the cars. 'AN' I DON'T NEED NO BOOT-LICKERS 'ROUND HERE, NEITHER!'

"The folks in their cars see all the guns on the back of Bubba's truck; they roll up their windows and start easin' on outta there. I figured those folks all feared God to some extent, but that morning they were in no hurry to get into Heaven.

"Bubba says, 'Sorry, good buddy. Gotta go.' An' he drives off."

Bugs rests his forearms on his thighs, like he's back at the scene. "Now I'm sitting' there in the rain, rear tires hangin' in the air over that dang ditch. So, I hop back in, turn over the engine, and it runs! But the steerin' wheel's bent, and I'm wonderin' if this thing'll even drive. So, I put it in gear and the rear wheels start spinnin' in the air over the ditch, and I think, 'This is good!'"

His truck is stuck in a ditch, his back tires are hanging in the air, his steering wheel is bent, his windshield is broken—and this is good?

"So now all I need is to get the truck outta that ditch."

That's all *he needs?*

"So, I put 'er in four-wheel drive, and just drove 'er outta there."

Sure. Easy as making flapjacks.

Bugs leans back in his camp chair and downs more beer. "So, I get goin' down the road, but the frame's bent, so now I'm only able to make left turns. I hate when that happens."

"Me, too," I say in solidarity.

"Lucky for me all the turns were to the left, 'cept for the right turn onto my property. So, when I got there, I just reversed it and kept turning left to back it in—mountain style."

I didn't quite follow the geometry of that last "mountain" maneuver, but, clearly, he got his truck home.

"So, what did you do about that bent frame?" I ask.

"Oh," says Bugs, "I just chained it between some trees with come-alongs and then whanged down on the ratchets till it straightened a bit. Dang thing drives a little sideways now, but it goes."

"Looks like it all turned out okay," I said.

"Yup. That's the Ozarks."

Bugs's version of life makes me almost long for those policy meetings and quarterly reports. He sets down his last empty can and stands to leave.

"Good talkin' with ya."

"Me, too. So long."

And with that, Bugs walks soundlessly toward the formless background and dissolves back into his dimension.

I take the last sip of my beer, add another log to the fire, and lean back, trying to picture Bugs's far-away world. *Is that even real?* The only world I feel certain of is the one I am sitting in. And then I notice my cooler is missing only one beer—the one in my hand.

The Path to Happiness

by Meredith S. Martin

Gemma grumbled as she watched her eleven-year-old brother Adam and his classmates having a high time at the school Halloween party. *How did she get roped into being a chaperone again this year?* Thirty ghosts, witches, and various other forms of supernatural creatures filled the gym at Warton Elementary School. They were shrieking like banshees while taking a turn at submerging their faces in a bucket filled with water and apples. Gemma felt like someone was inside her skull banging pots and pans together.

Gemma is considered to be a pretty girl. She is not too short and not too tall. Thick, curly brown hair silhouettes her almond skin and emphasizes green flecked hazel eyes. The only thing lacking from making her the picture-perfect girl nextdoor is her smile—she doesn't have one. Gemma can best be described as a nineteen-year-old shrew.

"Amy," she called out sharply, "take over for a few minutes, I need some air! I'll be right back." And with that, she turned and stalked out into the inky black night lighted only by the oval golden moon and some fireflies blinking cheerfully like little stop lights in the nearby woods. *What are they so darn happy about*, she thought. *Don't they know they're becoming extinct?*

But the fireflies fascinated her with their patterned dance in the warm night air; so she began to follow them as they illuminated the path leading through the woods. She had only gone a short distance when the woods opened up to a clearing toward the crest of the hill. She was in St. Thomas Churchyard and Cemetery. The fireflies circled around the tombstones and flickered a silent welcome.

Upon reaching the cemetery, she was somewhat startled to see a man sitting on a tombstone staring at the moon. Layers of fog cut only by shards of moonlight shrouded him lending a ghostly effect to the scene. Gemma was curious and not faint of heart. She was not going to be deterred by this eerie setting.

"What are you doing here by yourself in the middle of the night sitting on a tombstone?" she demanded.

"I am just immersing myself in the beauty of the night while wrapping myself in the cloak of happiness," he replied.

"But why here in this cemetery? Surely you have better places to be."

"Actually, I rather like it here. It has become my home away from home, you see."

"I don't understand, how could a cemetery be your home away from home?"

"Because I'm dead and this is my grave. But on October 31st when the vail between your world and mine is the thinnest, I can slip back into yours and enjoy the simple things of life like this beautiful night."

Gemma studied the tombstone's epitaph. *Robert J. Manahan; born July 17, 1936. Died August 2, 1989. He worked hard, died young, but provided well for his family.*

"What does that mean, Mr. Manahan?" queried Gemma.

"Just Bob to you, little lady. It means I worked almost every day of my life. I made lots of money. I used to study my bank account every day and figure out ways to make more money. Nothing was more important to me than making money but while I was making all that money, I forgot to go to my son's baseball game and my daughter's prom. I even forgot to bring my wife flowers for her birthday. I forgot lots of things. I did not realize what the important things in life were. I did not know what happiness was or where to look for it—but now I do. It just took dying for me to find it."

Openmouthed, Gemma sucked in her breath, then let it out in a gush. "Mr. Manahan—Bob—I am only nineteen years old but most of the time I am just angry or sad. For whatever reason, I cannot seem to be happy. I feel grumpy and miserable—I don't know what to do to enjoy life. Help me! Can you tell me how you found happiness? I don't want to have to die to find it."

"I can't tell you how to be happy. I wish I could. I can only show you a path to take. Everyone must discover it for themselves. Happiness is unique to each person. It is not just a feeling; it is a state of mind. It does not matter if you are rich or poor. It doesn't even depend on your health. I have encountered departed souls who said they were happy even when they learned they had a terminal illness. No, happiness is elusive, but I have faith that you will find it." Upon saying that, Bob gently reached out and placed a small package in her hand. "Don't open this until you get back to the party." And then in a wisp of fog he disappeared.

Shaking with anticipation, Gemma fairly flew back to the school. She stepped inside the vacant cloakroom and tore the wrappings off the package like a frenzied mad woman. Inside was just a small pentagon shaped mirror with a wavy three-dimensional appearance like that of a limpid pool. No note, no sage instructions, nothing—just a mirror. *What kind of joke is this?* She picked it up and gazed into it transfixed for what seemed like an eternity. Suddenly and without warning, she felt she was being sucked into her own reflection like Alice down the rabbit hole. Everything around her seemed to fade, whirl, and spin as though she was on a Tilt-A-Whirl. She was being pulled deeper and deeper into the mirror. Her chest tightened and her breathing was labored. She began to panic.

But as quickly as it started, it abruptly stopped. She had the sensation that she was floating upon an ethereal fluffy cloud. Gemma could feel her whole demeanor change, and like in the tale of the proverbial mustard seed, she began to have faith. She thought of her gentle loving parents who always had her back and she smiled. Adam popped into her mind with his puppy dog allegiance hanging on her every word. The smile grew wider and bigger. She felt a glow of contentment spread throughout her body like a warm river. It was then she understood what Bob was trying to show her. Gemma was experiencing a new, strange feeling—Gemma was happy!

The mirror began to glow translucent white like a halo. She peeked at it. It reflected herself—Gemma—with a big beautiful smile.

"Thank you, Bob. I understand what you were trying to show me; it has been there all the time. I am on my path to happiness. I know that it is a slippery path and I may slide off now and then, but I am determined to get back on again. And maybe—just maybe I will be privileged enough to show others how to discover it for themselves."

Stop Reading—Now!

by Robert E. Marvin

Midge Wright ignored the sleet peppering the small office window on the thirteenth floor of the Randolph Building. She opened the next brown envelope in the pile of short story entries. She massaged the bridge of her nose and poured another diet cola. The sign on her office door read, Midge Wright—Assistant Editor—Barnhill Press. Assistant flunky and resident pain in the ass are what Blanch, the woman who occupied the next cubicle, called her.

She thought she should be having dinner uptown, finishing her second, or maybe third Harvey Wallbanger instead of wading through this pile of trash.

Without an immediate boost in sagging revenue there would be new tenants here within a month. In a panic, she had pitched the idea of a short story contest to the managing editor, Ian Strong.

She told him each entry would bring in a ten-dollar entry fee, and every winner would be sure to buy the special edition containing the winning stories and extras for easily impressed friends and family.

She read,

> Rance plopped down on the red divan and looked longingly into—

She tossed the entry into the trash. *One more disastrous load of trash, and I'm going out to get wasted.*

A priority mail envelope waved from the middle of the pile. She slipped it out, tore it open, exhaled slowly, and prepared for the inevitable disappointment.

> Have you ever read something that never should have been written?

She swiveled her chair around and propped her feet on her lower desk drawer. *I'd kill for a foot massage.*
She read on.

> I had to send this manuscript to someone. This story should never have been written. I fell into a sort of trance. When I awoke, the manuscript lay before me with a page warning that anyone who read it would descend into hell. It also said that I would suffer the same fate if I didn't pass the story to someone.

It is somewhat intriguing.
The story continued.

> I beg you, stop reading! The most terrible things will happen to you unless you lock it away where no one will ever find it. Please do not—ever—read this story and don't contact me—ever!

The signature was shakily written. But years of reading entry writers' dreadful handwriting made recognizing the name Bomar Alsheer easy.
Midge's stomach growled. *All right; we'd have to alter the opening a bit, but I'm sufficiently intrigued to read this later.*
She opened her briefcase, slid the manuscript in, and snapped the cover closed. She punched a button on her phone. "Al, get me a cab! She heard Al mumble an obscene response before he hung up.
She hit the *L* key on the elevator keypad. The doors closed, and it gave an unusual lurch as it headed down. Her purse slipped down to her wrist spilling the contents onto the floor. "Damn it!"

She had managed to retrieve everything by the time the door opened onto the lobby.

She walked past Al and out the door. The sleet had turned to snow, and it blew against her face. She squinted. At least the cab was on time.

"Café l'Europe."

The driver flipped the meter and, uncharacteristically, said nothing.

Thirty minutes later, she ordered a Caesar salad, a rare steak, and a double vodka martini. *Thank God it's still happy hour.* She was used to eating alone. Still, it was almost Christmas, and this season she had nothing to look forward to except work. Her fourth relationship had ended every bit as badly as her second and third.

Café l'Europe was the type of place where men took women who weren't their wives for romantic dinners before they headed to her apartment for the inevitable. She only came here when her affairs ended badly, and they always did. Either the men tired of her or, in the case of the only one she really loved, he suddenly died.

Several hours, two more martinis, and a Harvey Wallbanger later she lay curled up in bed with the late news playing on her new 52" TV system. "You've put on a couple of pounds Eddie," she said to the local newsman. He had been affair number three.

She muted the sound, rolled on her side, and retrieved the manuscript from her brief case. She needed to find something worthy of a prize or she'd be out on the street.

She adjusted her pillow. She flipped to the title page. The Story That Should Never Be Read by Bomar Alsheer. There was no return envelope, just the story.

The first line read,

For the love of God, you must stop reading!

Yeah, right.

> This is a tale about some very evil things that have not
> happened. They will only happen if you read the story
> written below. You will determine if these terrible things
> happen to you.

It was a clever way to begin a story and a good hook. It had kept her reading. Still, there was something creepy about all this. Yet she was not in the least superstitious. Nevertheless, she felt apprehension and uneasiness. *Too many drinks*, she told herself.

She got up, went into the kitchen, and got a bottle of Evian out of the fridge. She had it half gone by the time she was back in bed. *This is ridiculous. It's an entry in a short story contest. Just read the damn thing and get it over with.*

It was the best thing so far, and if she didn't come up with something actually worth printing, she could be out on her ass. She had used up too many chances already, so she continued to read.

> This is a story of how souls are harvested for the city of the damned. It will show you how easy it is for the living to be fooled by the evil ones. Their souls are sucked from their bodies, which do not die, but become soulless hulks, unable to move or speak.

There was a *tap—tap* at her window, and she jumped. Nervously, she eased over to the window. It was slightly ajar. The sleet had started again. *Dumb ass!*

She picked up the manuscript and continued reading.

> A person, even a good person, can have her soul sucked out by the terrible words of this story. I begged you to stop reading! Now it is too late for you! You should have listened when you could have stopped reading. Now your soul will be in eternal darkness, tormented night and day by the demons of the story. They will feed on every bit of joy, every good memory, until there is nothing left but everlasting despair.

Her eyes widened as she read on. Panic pounded her brain. Her heart crashed against her collapsing lungs, but her eyes would not be pulled away from the words. Terror ravaged her every nerve as she reached the final line. Her last gasp caught in her throat as her lips spoke her last sane words. "*Exsercrari esse!*"

These words drifted off as a soft voice spoke, "Goodbye Midge Wright." Her eyes closed and contorted with an effort to scream.

The TV blinked on into the night, its surround sound muted like Midge's cries.

In the morning the alarm would go off, but no one would hear it. Midge wouldn't have a breakfast bagel at the East End Coffee Shop, call a taxi, report to work, nor start another affair, not that morning—not any morning.

The wind blew the window wide open. The story flew off the bed and rolled under Midge's dresser.

In the weeks that followed, her things at the office were packed into two large boxes and sent to the extended care facility where Midge lay comatose. No visitor would ever come to see her. Soon everything she owned would be sold to pay for her care. A court would order her life support terminated. But, to the astonishment of the doctors, she wouldn't die.

A man from Delaware would buy her condo. One day in the spring he would lose a cufflink and, searching under the dresser, he would pick up a dusty manuscript and reach for his reading glasses.

Finding My Direction

by Mark H. Newhouse

Shiny with the snow of night, Pa's boots leave spreading puddles on the raw floorboards. "Try me on," they taunt—laces: limp worms. I don't dare.

Pa trudged through the snow after a night of drink at the bar. He'll be in a foul temper in the morning, awakin' to snow-covered fields.

Pa's boots . . . tossed down . . . he didn't bother settin' them upright. I set the ungiving rubber soles flat on the floor. Their open mouths tease, "Boy, you ain't never gonna fit in your pa's shoes." They look mighty large from the view of a boy barely more than a sprout.

"Your ma's shoes was always paired up neat," Pa says when something pops up to remind him of her. "Them half-dozen pairs of lady shoes stood in a line like little soldiers waitin' on inspection." He let out once he couldn't figure how Ma's tiny footwear left no room for his one pair of combat boots. He kept them as spit-shined reminders of his "glory days." He never wore 'em once . . . insisted they be "preserved" in the closet he ceded to Ma. "She was a mystery to me, your little mama," he mumbles and shuts the closet door . . . shuts in her reminders.

It took three years after Ma passed before Pa packed up her things in burlap sacks. There was tears in his eyes. He tried to cover 'em up. Some things you can't hide.

The best times on our farm are when seeding or harvesting keeps Pa's mind occupied. He used to heft me up to the tractor seat. "You're king of our *blessed land*," Pa would say and chuckle. When we was done with chores, he would say, "Thank you, sonny." I was just settin' next to him, doing nothing. At dusk, purple and red ribbons streaked the sky.

I scampered to keep up with his big black boots. I longed to fill them monsters in which he strutted. Hungry, I'd see stars poking through the black sheet of night as I skipped mud puddles by walking in his giant footprints. Someday, I'll be a giant. Nobody whips a giant.

I am not afraid of Pa when the crops chain his hands to the tractor. Things change when the chill air pens us indoors . . . turns him into a trapped animal without Ma to tame him. Winter for Pa is like the full moon to werewolves in horror movies. With flames blazing in the fireplace he built for her from dug-up boulders, smoke carries the smell of charred wood. He paces the rug. He barely ever settles in his chair . . . gets raw tempered. He stares through the frosty panes of the window for hours. At times, he darts fiery eyes at me, mumbles about seein' Ma's ghost-eyes in the icy glass.

I look.

No such luck.

It's a blessing when Pa trucks out at night . . . leaves me on my own. Settin' by the fire, I watch flames chew on the logs. The pop and crackle hush out all other sounds. The burning wood gives off a bacon smell that fills the room. Warms the place up. Emptiness soothes . . . like if Pa was gone too.

The raw wood planks no longer hold the outline of Ma's galoshes. I can't remember her face. Only seen it in a photograph Pa keeps in his drawer. Caught him gazing at it one night. He run his finger over the glass . . . shot his red-streaked eyes to me. Drunk, stumblin' tryin' to stand, belt hanging half-off his jeans, Pa rasped, "You killed her, boy! You killed your mama."

Pa's words knifed through me worse than when the belt danglin' in his hand strikes my butt. I shouted back, "Is it my damn fault I was born?"

"You talkin' back to me?" Pa raised the belt.

I didn't dare sass him whilst he was stinkin' of alcohol, hefting that thick leather belt with brass buckle. Besides, Pa had a point. Ma met her Maker when I was dropped into the world, in the midst of a blizzard. Pa did not need to lay blame on me. I done enough of that myself.

At night, when I hear his truck return after a binge, I hightail it to bed . . . lock my eyes tight. At times, I hear hushed sounds from his room. I imagine the punishment he's administerin' to one of them cheap town women. Nothin' I can do about it. Just grateful in the mornin' whoever he cajoled into his bed is gone. I do not want to meet up with black-and-blue arms and worse. Streaked makeup and smudged lipstick are hard enough. At least the women he brings get away. I will. Someday. I dream about leaving . . . mostly after the outbursts . . . when I see Ma as his hand falls.

I was twelve and seven months. I was up before dawn. The tree branches sagged under snow blankets. Thick wool socks, two layers, I slid a foot into Pa's wet boot. Just tryin' them on. Too large, even with double socks on my feet. Nobody yellin', I dropped my other foot into the moist flannel throat of the other boot. "Almost fit," I gushed to Ma's ghost.

I caught her smile in the windowpane.

I inched up the door hasp. A glance at Pa's locked room and I squeezed through the part-open door. Closed it quick . . . keep the icy air from waking him. He come in late and alone. Little chance he'd wake.

Once off the porch, I bent over, tied his laces in double knots . . . to keep the boots from falling off. Feet barely keeping his boots on, I trudged across the lawn, fightin' for each step in the snow and harsh wind.

My steps on the icy lawn echoed loud in my ears.

Crunch. Crunch.

My eyes shot to his window.

No light.

No face peering. No hand wiping the glass.

A thin slice of light . . . a distance ahead.

"That damn town," Pa grumbles, "is crawling closer to our blessed land each year. Soon, we'll have nothing left for you to inherit. Damn shame."

In the ice-cold, clear sky, I could almost touch the line of light with my finger. "It ain't far," I said, jerkin' Pa's boot out of the snow and pushing ahead.

"Boy, what the hell you doing?"

I froze in place. My imagination? The wind makin' noise? He's drunk . . . fast asleep.

"You get yourself in here, boy. You ain't never going to be big enough to fill my boots." He yelled louder, "You get them man boots back here afore I takes a strap to your ass. I'll do it. You know that."

My feet felt lost in his boots, even with laces tied tight as I can. I shivered. Not from the chill air. Not too late to turn back . . . might escape the belt. Come up with an excuse, "I was just gettin' a head start

. . . fetchin' eggs before the freeze." His beating ain't that bad. Hurt my pride more than my butt.

"Boy, do you hear me?"

I pivoted around. Pa was barefoot. He didn't have no spares . . . only them army boots . . . won't wear them in snow. I turned my head. The city lights . . . just across the field.

"What the hell is wrong with you? Get my damn boots in here! Now!"

Ma's voice come to me, "Pa can't catch you in bare feet. You got time. Run!"

Crunch, crunch. Two more steps.

"Where you goin,' fool?"

I'd run . . . his boots woulda' come clean-off. "Look at them lights. You can make it," Ma says. "From the depot, the Greyhound will take you anywhere in the world."

"You want a whipping?"

I stopped walkin,' not facing him, not wantin' Pa to see me tremblin'. The boots felt too big. The rising sun dimming the town lights . . . barely saw them in the haze.

"We'll forget this happened. I forgive you."

I stared at the pitiful being he'd become. My footprints trailing from the house were filling with snow. On the horizon, the city lights, like the night stars, were disappearin' as the sun rose. The way forward was buried . . . no clear paths.

"You can't escape. You ain't got the guts."

No path. No guts? I can't make it.

"Yes, you can," Ma's voice cut through the howling wind. "Yes, you can do anything you want."

My boots felt tighter as I trudged against the blinding snow toward the town lights.

The Recliner

by Donna Parrey

Who buys a nubby tweed recliner as a wedding gift for her twenty-seven-year-old husband? I did. And the way Ben's eyes lit up when he stepped into our new condo and saw it, I was lucky he didn't drop the white-gowned bundle he was carrying over the threshold.

When we were dating, my efficiency sported two fuzzy bean bag chairs—one coral and one teal—in front of the TV: a set-up he tolerated because he loved me. Ben's apartment had a leather couch which I thought was too cold and he thought was too hot. The sixty-second commercials for the Bentley Relax-away recliner practically had him drooling.

Ben and the tweed Bentley were a match made in Heaven. The recliner had a plastic cup holder on the left arm that worked well for my southpaw. There was also a lined pocket on the left flank to stow the remote control and the *TV Guide Magazine*. On the right was a long wooden lever that simultaneously raised the footpad and lowered the back. He'd yank it as if he were shifting into gear at the start of the Indy 500, launching himself into what he came to call "chillax mode."

We "broke it in" the first day back from our honeymoon. The recliner wasn't designed for that kind of activity, and our chests heaved together, fueled more by laughter than lust. It became a sacred ritual for all celebrations, including the creation of our two children—three years and five years after our wedding.

The official color of the recliner, per its sales receipt, was Green/Brown. I liked to think of it as Nature's Blend. Our kids called it "Rotten Avocado." He called it "perfect." Coffee, salsa, even gravy had a way of embracing, perhaps even enhancing, the weave, without causing guests to raise their eyebrows.

The decades passed. The kids grew up and moved out. The tweed grew threadbare in symmetrical spots. But there was never a thought of relocating, refurbishing, or replacing the recliner. It was a mainstay of our living room and our life. It became his primary repository after he took ill. Ben wanted out of the hospital as quickly as possible, and when the doctors finally suggested hospice, he was adamant that he wished to "chillax to death" at home.

He did.

The weeks and months that followed left me numb. I operated on autopilot, paying bills, taking out the garbage, replacing the soured milk with fresh. Whenever the kids and their families visited, they'd gently advise me to let the recliner go. My five-year-old granddaughter pronounced it most elegantly: "Get rid of it, Nana!" I knew it was unhealthy to keep it as a shrine of sorts. I couldn't bear to sit in it. I simply circled around the recliner on my way from one room to the next, eyeing it with a heaviness of spirit each time I passed.

One day I felt the need to connect with Ben so badly that I allowed myself to gingerly sink onto the recliner's cushion, its fabric as warm as if he had just risen. I leaned back, closed my eyes, gripped the wooden lever, and pulled it back. Gently. Not an instant launch into chillax mode but a slow somber descent into a place I hadn't inhabited in years.

My brain cells scattered wildly about, eventually settling like grains of sand in the undertow, pulling me along to depths I wasn't ready for. Away. Away. I heard what sounded like a howling wind but I felt no breeze. An intense brightness forced me to squeeze my eyelids tighter. When the discomfort abated, I dared to unclench my facial muscles. My eyelids lifted to reveal an ethereal blue fog surrounding me. Just a few yards away, I saw the silhouette of a figure approaching. The fog dispersed. It was Ben.

"Hey, babe! I've been waiting for you."

I tried to respond. I attempted to rise from the recliner. All of my faculties were in a state of numbness. Deep within my brain I was crying and reaching for Ben, but my body remained perfectly still, cradled in the recliner.

"Don't worry . . . you're in chillax mode right now. But I needed you to come; I have things to say that you need to hear. Babe, I am so, so grateful for the life we had together. You gave me a love that lasted, and we made two great kids that grew into adults we could be proud of. And they gifted us grandchildren! Our family needs you to come back, to see you smile again. I may have had to leave sooner than I ever anticipated, but you . . . you still have decades in front of you. I know you'll never forget me, and I'm not asking you to. I'm simply telling you that it is time for you to carry on. Bring a new love into your life. I want to see you happy again. You deserve it, and so do I. If I felt like my passing ended your life as well, I couldn't bear the sorrow. Go back. Laugh at our memories. Embrace the kiddos. Enjoy everything that life has to offer. And donate that recliner to Goodwill! I love you, babe. You can do this!"

A sense of peace permeated my being. As Ben faded back into the blue fog, my brain once again swirled me into a bright tunnel that abruptly ended with a soft thud. I cautiously re-opened my eyes and regained focus. I was back in my living room, lying on our old tweed Bentley.

I won't say it was easy, but I took Ben's words to heart. The kids were pleased the next time they visited and the old recliner was gone. In its place sat a Queen Anne chair and a small bookcase at its side. I joined a neighborhood book club. I discovered a new thrift shop. I started attending yoga classes.

It was another year before I went on my first date. I met Jeffrey in a bookstore, and he asked me out for coffee. Another time, we went kayaking. Oh, and we tried that new Italian restaurant on Grand Street. He even enjoys antiquing with me at flea markets. Last week we visited Second Chance Antiques and Bric-a-Brac Shoppe. While I was examining a nifty set of ceramic bookends, I heard Jeffrey exclaim, "Well, I'll be . . . check out this vintage Bentley Relax-away!"

The Commitment

by William R. Platt

I met my husband on October 10, 2035, in the main banquet hall of the Altamonte Hilton. The room was packed with people waiting to hear the keynote speaker. I found an empty seat in the back.

"Is this chair taken?" I asked.

My future husband looked at me with those gorgeous brown eyes. "It is now, my friend," he said. "My name is Phil Watkins. I'm in robotics."

"Nice to meet you. Dave Campbell, astro-biologist with Waytheon."

Electricity shot up and down my spine when we shook hands.

"How long have you been with Waytheon?" he asked.

"Fifteen years, ever since I graduated from Cal Tech."

It was the beginning of a conversation that has never ended.

Four months later, I moved into Phil's bungalow near Cape Canaveral. It was supposed to be a trial period. After all, we're scientists; we always test our hypotheses. Three months later, we married in a private ceremony.

Our marriage isn't all butterflies and rainbows. Sometimes we quarrel over the TV, but not too often. One truly legendary fight came a year after the wedding. I found a Pomeranian puppy in a shelter and fell in love. I even named her Pepper hoping to instantly make her part of our family. Phil wouldn't budge.

"We're not ready," he said.

"She's a dog. How ready do we have to be?"

"I'm not ready. It's a big commitment. A dog has to be fed. It needs shots and to go for walks. I'm too busy."

No matter how often I offered to take sole responsibility for Pepper, Phil wouldn't have it. I moped around the house for weeks.

Phil wasn't joking about being busy. He works nonstop in freelance robotics. He has a genius for innovation. It's not unusual to come home and find Phil poring over schematics with an Air Force Colonel or SpaceX engineers. Some companies have offered him millions, but he's stubborn. He likes the quiet life with limited interruptions.

Behind our little house is a two-story structure originally built as a stable. The previous owners converted it to a garage and then Phil turned it into his workshop. Sometimes he disappears for days, even sleeping upstairs on a cot. Much of his work is classified "Top Secret." Access without twenty-four-hour notification is strictly forbidden.

One night, Phil emerged from seclusion carrying a cardboard box.

"I've got a surprise for you," he said, setting the box on the floor.

As I bent down, something shook the box from the inside and issued three high-pitched barks. A furry little bundle of energy with big brown eyes and a pink tongue hopped into my arms. I hugged her to my face and let the kissing begin.

"Pepper! How did you find her?"

"She's not Pepper, but she's as close as I could make her."

"What?"

Phil bit his lower lip.

"I made her, Dave. She's a robot."

"No, she's not. Look how excited she is."

Phil pointed to my bookshelves. "I read about neuronal populations in the cerebral cortex. It's just nano-circuitry between the hypothalamus, amygdala—

"Yes," I interrupted, "I know the biological origins of emotions, but, come on, this is a real dog."

Phil bit his lip. "Press the gemstone in the collar."

I pressed the button. Pepper curled into a ball and went to sleep on my lap.

"Press it again," said Phil.

Pepper shook her head, rubbed her eyes with her paws, and yipped when she saw me.

"My God, what have you done."

"I made you a dog, Dave, only better. You don't have to feed her or clean up after her, and she'll last longer."

"How long?"

"We can recharge her batteries, but eventually they'll wear out."

"I can't believe this. You've created life."

"No, she's a machine. But don't tell anybody, not even my dad. People are funny about these things."

It didn't take long to get used to a furry little robot running around the place. Pepper barks at strangers, chases squirrels, and sleeps at the end of the bed. She's my little PepperPot. I can't imagine being without her.

Adjusting to Phil's father was more difficult. Conrad Watkins is a florist from West Texas. I met him when I came home from work one evening and found a stranger sitting at our kitchen table with a laptop.

"Who are you?"

"Hello, I'm Conrad Watkins, Phil's father." He rose and extended his hand. The physical similarities between father and son were striking.

"Mr. Watkins, hello, I'm David. So nice to finally meet you." He seemed not to notice my invitation for a hug, so I took his hand and shook it warmly. "When did you get in?"

"An hour ago."

"You should have let us know. I would have taken the day off."

"I called Phil this morning from Atlanta. No need to take time off from your job. I'm only here for a few days."

"Where's Phil?"

"Working."

With that, Conrad sat back down and immersed himself in his laptop. That thirty-second conversation summarizes our relationship.

Conrad went home four days later, leaving behind a vase full of daisies on the kitchen table. This pattern repeats every couple of years.

Late one night, I found Pepper lying in the hallway. Her eyes were open and her tongue sticking out the side of her mouth. I pressed the button on the collar. Nothing happened. I scooped her up and raced toward Phil's workshop.

"Phil, something's wrong with Pepper!"

I pounded on the wooden garage door. A high-pitched motor whirred from deep inside. I pounded harder.

No answer. I kicked the bottom of the door. It wobbled on its hinges. I pulled it open and went in.

Silhouetted in fiery light, Phil hunched at his workbench. He wore thick gloves and a welder's helmet as sparks flew from a grinding wheel.

"Phil! It's Pepper!"

He didn't respond. I put a hand on his shoulder. He jumped at the touch and looked at me through dark lenses. He snapped off the grinder and lifted his helmet. It was Conrad.

"Hello, David."

I stumbled. "Conrad? What are you doing here?"

"Dave?" Phil was behind me. "What's wrong with Pepper?" He took her stiff body from my arms and attached a power cord inside her ear. "Her battery needs recharging. She'll be okay."

"What's he doing here?" I jabbed a finger at Conrad.

Phil bit his lip. "Conrad is always here."

"What do you mean? He's your dad from Texas!"

"No, he's a robot, like Pepper, but more sophisticated. I built him. Someday, I hope to inhabit Conrad's body with my persona."

Conrad remained perfectly still, his eyes following me as I examined him. I could almost hear the servos and circuits buzzing with electricity.

"I'm having problems grafting my emotions onto his processors, but I'm close, Dave, very close. Then you and I can be together forever."

"You're turning yourself into a robot? Phil, that's crazy. What about me? I don't want to be a machine."

Phil chewed on his lip. "There's something else, Dave." He paused, looking for the right words. "You know how Pepper doesn't eat or defecate? She's not the only one in our family with those traits."

Comprehension came slowly. "You're saying I'm a robot?"

"What did you have for breakfast today?"

I thought back and found a blank spot.

"What about lunch or dinner?"

Nothing came to mind.

"You can't remember because there's nothing to remember. You don't miss it because your programming won't permit it."

"That's impossible. People would notice."

"Think about it. There are people you've known for years, but you've never seen them eat and you certainly don't follow them into the bathroom."

"My childhood memories. Mom and Dad. The car accident."

"Those are constructs programmed into your software. I'm sorry, Dave. Everything before your inception date is a fabrication."

"My inception date?"

"October 10, 2035."

"The convention, the day we met?"

Phil nodded.

Over time, I learned to accept who and what I am. I used to have an off button, but that's no longer necessary. Now I hook into the system to recharge my batteries or install an upgrade.

Phil downloaded himself into Conrad's body. Every so often, he performs some surgical magic to keep us looking the proper age. Pepper is outside chasing squirrels. We've been together for eighty years. Life is good.

Rocking High

by Barbara Ryan

Before I die, I have a tale to tell from long ago. It's a true story—I think—and a mystery, for sure, reported here to the best of my recollection.

New Year's Eve, 1978

We ran on fumes after a five-night concert series, capped off by a midnight blowout at Winterland Ballroom in San Francisco. Not only was this the conclusion of our year-long tour, but it also marked the final night for Winterland, originally an ice rink but now aging, with plaster falling from its high ceiling. Still, it was a venerable concert hall that every rock band had to play at least once. Several concert films were made there, including *The Last Waltz*, The Band's Thanksgiving 1976 final concert filmed by Martin Scorsese, and *The Closing of Winterland*, the Grateful Dead event this story is about.

San Francisco, my hometown, growing up and out. I was searching for something, and here's what I found: Haight-Ashbury, late '60s, marijuana highs, LSD, hippies, druggies, rock 'n' roll—you name it, anything goes. War resisters, draft dodgers, Vietnam. Why are we there? Why are we dying? Why are we killing? Dude, fight back. Say no. I said no, no way, man. Time to drop out. That became my new direction, where I'm coming from now, and why I lost it in music, my new dimension. Zone to flatline, hear the voices, put it out, take it in, feel the pull.

This was it—the last concert, end of an era. We occupied the hall until the doors closed. We started at midnight and served breakfast at 5.00 a.m. It was a happening.

But before breakfast, around 3:00 a.m., Bob Weir called out to me, "Jerry." I opened my eyes, saw Bob's raised eyebrows and questioning look, and noticed strange sounds and sights. We didn't know what it was or how to respond. Here's what happened.

During the twenty-five-minute set of "Fire on the Mountain/Scarlet Begonias," the two of us spotted chartreuse aliens. We looked at each other, but neither of us said anything because we thought it was the weed and the hallucinations that sometimes accompany it. That didn't stop us, despite ghost-dancing lasers darting around the band. We almost quit playing when we saw the abduction of our drummer, Mickey Hart, even as the drumsticks continued to strike the drum. Then, while I was singing, my mouth opened wide, and notes floated out—no sound, just musical notes dancing in the wind.

By 4:00 a.m., some audience members began screaming and howling, but no one noticed. Our concerts always had animated audience participation. Bob and I saw the chartreuse figures carry off some of these very fans. Everyone else in the band and the audience gave no response. They didn't notice the bizarre sights and sounds that we did. So, like, it still had to be the weed. Right?

When the green apparitions took Bob, my senses were fully alert: "I'm next."

My eyes scanned the other band members and the audience, but no one showed any signs of anything strange. We continued to play. Nothing was unusual about the audience jumping and singing along— it simply indicated that Bob and I weren't the only ones smoking grass. We're known as the psychedelic rock band of the nation. Phil Lesh and Mickey Hart had been smoking too, but maybe we were the only ones smoking bad grass. Yeah, man, that was it.

Nothing to do but keep playing. Stop thinking, maybe.

My fear of being taken proved unfounded. By 5:00 a.m., the alien creatures had vanished, and all band members and absent fans were back in their places as if nothing unusual had occurred over the last two hours. Mentioning it would reveal lost consciousness—something I wasn't willing to do, even though I hoped that was what had happened. It turned out no green extraterrestrials had hauled off audience members after all.

But the odd thing was that the fans never stopped screaming and dancing, even as they couldn't stop eating. They were ravenous for the champagne, ham, and eggs. Grossly exaggerated chewing with mouths wide open, saliva running down their chins. Weed again, don't you think?

Strange occurrences began after that final concert at Winterland. Some fans traveled hundreds of miles to attend shows and festivals wherever we performed, calling themselves Deadheads. Their reputation was as heavy drug users because they got high during performances and developed new slang and idioms. Before each concert, they set up tables selling tie-dyed T-shirts, stickers, buttons, tapes, posters, and other paraphernalia. They created a counterculture. Alongside those tables was one called Wharf Rats, named after one of our songs, established to support fans who didn't use drugs but were uplifted by the music alone.

Some Deadheads became activists for social change, particularly regarding the environment. Many had previously protested the Vietnam War and the draft, which sent young men to kill and die for people they didn't know and who had done nothing to them. They also continued their support for women's equality, Black civil rights, Native American and Chicano movements, gay liberation, and union organizing. Some became supporters for the first time. These causes were noble, and we were pleased to see our fans fighting for significant issues. We supported them too. Primarily, though, we sang about enjoying life, getting high, and creating an alternative American experience. The core ethos of our songs was freedom and openness to exploration and change. Long hair and beards symbolized rebellion, a quest for a new direction and way of life.

That night in Winterland told its tale. Transformation. Was it the drugs, or did the aliens infect us and our followers? No one knew where the Deadheads, Wharf Rats, or counterculture came from, except Bob knows, and I know.

And we'll never tell.

Terms

by H.G. Silvia

Colin stepped back from his father's gravestone, turning up his collar against the lingering winter chill. Father preached, *Take no risks. Stay the course* for a trouble-free life. But Father never had to explain blight to a hungry child or when they might eat again. In his day, their valley was bountiful and taken for granted. What would Father think today?

"Colin?" A small voice called above the biting wind.

He turned. "Father was wrong, Sister."

Fiona's ashen face matched the overcast sky. "They all were. But only we suffer for it."

"I've made my decision. I leave at sunrise." Colin watched her face for acceptance but found only sorrow.

"And when you don't return?" Tears welled.

"One less mouth to feed."

"One less man to protect us. To see that food's shared equally."

"That won't be enough. Someone must leave the valley and find a solution before the stores run dry. Dry, dead husks litter our fields. Nothing grows here, now."

Fiona's face hardened. "No man has ever come back."

"If I don't try, I am no man."

Colin hoisted an empty pack over his shoulder and stepped into the morning light. The townsfolk stood between him and his trek. They'd debated what to do for so long, fear crippled them.

"I trust you haven't come to stop me." Colin scanned their faces.

A small boy pushed his way through the murmuring crowd and offered a folded rag. "It's not much, but you'll need strength for your journey."

Colin opened the offering and found nuts and a few dried berries. When he tried to refuse, the boy slipped away. Others stepped forward, each with small portions of what little food they could spare. Fiona was correct—no one had ever left the valley and come back. Everyone knew this, yet they willingly sacrificed their food to aid this folly.

Fiona stood beyond the crowd; her pale face wet with tears. "There must be another way." She trembled as he approached and took her in his arms. "I can't lose you, too."

"If I stay, we all lose." He kissed her head. "Light a candle for me, Sister. I will return."

Two days' walk behind him, he came to the southern entrance to the Cave of Lost Souls—the only assumed passage to the world beyond. A small sign lay askew against a stony outcropping. Colin brushed away the moss to reveal the carved words: Go Back.

"Wouldn't that make Father proud?" He muttered to no one.

He knelt, retrieved the torch from his pack, and set it ablaze with a flint. He welcomed the warmth on his face as he trod inside. Singing Father's song helped him pass the time while unseen creatures scurried away along the path. Bats above sang their shrill warnings. The odor of their droppings, mixed with the wet stone, assaulted his senses. The torch's flame danced against a warm, salty breeze from ahead. Two more verses rang out before he saw the light.

The cave opened to a great cavern. At its center, a massive, bottomless pool teeming with swirls of pale-blue light like nothing he'd ever seen or heard of.

"You were warned to go back," a voice boomed in the rocky space.

Colin's heart quickened; his grip tightened.

"Show yourself." Colin tried to project confidence despite weak knees and a light head.

"I'll tell you what I told the others: You are not worthy." The voice came from the darkness above.

Light and shadow drew strange shapes on the cave ceiling. By the far side, a shimmering thing moved against the light from the pool below.

He thought of Father's admonition again: *play it safe, risk nothing*. He also thought of Fiona's gaunt, gray face and the starving children who shared their last meals for this last hope.

Colin sucked in a deep breath of musty air, shook off his fear, and steeled himself. "It is *you* who are not worthy to look upon me."

The cavern filled with a deep, rumbling laughter, loud enough to send ripples through the illuminated pond. In the reflection, a shimmering, scaly neck descended, revealing a massive head with burning red eyes. With its graceful movement came the sound of tumbling coins. Beneath the beast, a substantial pile of gold and jewels. Nose to nose, Colin trembled but stood his ground.

"Why have you come all this way? Surely, there are easier ways to die." The beast's hot breath surrounded Colin.

"My people are starving. I seek only a way to save them."

The creature slid a clawed foot forward, raking gilded treasure into the pool. Gold sparkled as it sank through the light. "And you thought you could help yourself to my bounty?"

Colin gave thought and answered. "Have there been men before me?"

"Countless."

"Have any ever left this cave?"

The beast appeared thoughtful. "None."

"Then how would I know of your bounty?"

The beast recoiled his long neck at this logic, drawing his face away from Colin's. "Clever. But you are still but a man."

"What became of the others?" Colin asked but feared the answer.

"Each became entranced by my treasure, tried to bargain for it, but none could meet my terms. I did what I must to protect my secrets."

Colin understood where others' greed had failed them. "We cannot eat your treasure. It holds no value for us. I'll meet your terms if you help us."

The beast smiled at Colin's offer. "Your precious valley can be saved, but you will not like my terms."

Colin considered his people's fate: "I don't have to like them."

Faint screams carried on cool spring winds wrested Fiona from slumber. Colin's candle sat vigilantly in a north-facing window. She wrapped herself in a quilt and stepped outside. Toward the center of the village, an orange glow cast eerie shapes into a growing cloud of smoke. Something dark and immense interrupted the clouds. Smoke twirled at the edges of its outstretched leathery wings.

A dragon . . . come to finish us off?

As it approached Fiona's home, the beast bared its teeth, and with a hideous shriek, spewed white-hot streams of flames that engulfed what remained of the dry, lifeless crop fields.

The dragon circled, setting acre after acre ablaze.

Famine was just the beginning. We'll not live long enough to starve.

Smaller points of light crested the hill. Men with torches. Men with spears and crossbows. Coming to stop the destruction—to kill this beast.

They will die fighting. More noble than starving.

When the dragon finished its swailing, all the crop fields were razed, but the fires diminished quickly. Landing between Fiona and the fields, fiery eyes and a great black silhouette were all Fiona could discern of it. The beast shook the ground with each step toward her. Fiona knew her time had come to an end. She stood defiant as the beast encroached.

The dragon seemed focused on Colin's candle in her window.

"That was meant to guide my brother home. He's gone to save us all." She let out a defeated laugh. "He'll be the only one to have survived."

The mob of men circled the dragon, weapons at the ready. The beast paid them no mind.

Fiona saw the men and urged them closer. "Why have you come here, dragon? We are already dying. We have nothing for you here but death."

"I struck a bargain in a cave, and I came to fulfill my promises."

Fiona looked at the destruction. "What promises were those, devil?"

The dragon's gaze flitted from Colin's candle to Fiona's eyes. "To end our suffering."

Before he could say more, the men attacked. The beast didn't fight back, and in short order, he was felled. Fiona shouted her protest, but the men didn't relent until his bloody head lay dying in the soil.

Fiona approached, and the dragon spoke with ragged breaths. "Dragon's breath has cleansed our blight. New crops will grow from the ashes."

"*Our* suffering? *Our* blight? Colin? Why didn't you tell us this was you?"

"There were . . . terms, Fiona."

———

A cursed dragon can live only a day after leaving his den—his prison. Finding someone to meet his terms and take his place took eons. Into the world beyond, from The Cave of Lost Souls, a new man bearing Colin's face walked free. On his shoulder, he carried a pack heavy with coins.

A New Game for Travis

by K.L. Small

Mrs. Helen Willis sat across from the child psychologist, holding back her tears. "Travis still doesn't show any emotion."

"Your son's autism diagnosis indicates level-one severity," the psychologist said, reading from his computer screen. "Is he performing basic tasks at home without instruction?"

"Yes, but he's becoming more withdrawn," she said. Fearing a lonely, desperate future for him, she added, "My main concern is that he doesn't have any friends."

After a few more clicks on the keyboard, he locked eyes with her. "What does he do with his free time?"

"He watches one particular *Star Trek* episode over and over." She rubbed her forehead, thinking of the daily drone of the dialogue. She could repeat every word in the scene.

His fingers glided over the keyboard as he typed an entry. "Which one?"

"It's called 'Where No Man Has Gone Before.' He replays the part where Captain Kirk and Spock play a multi-level game that sort of looks like chess."

"Chess?" The psychologist raised an eyebrow and glanced at the digital clock on his desk. "Perhaps he would enjoy playing checkers."

The next day, Helen enrolled her ten-year-old son in the library's game club for kids. A week later, Travis sat across from a boy named Mason, a checkerboard between them. While the other parents browsed the library's book collection, Helen sat in the quiet game room in case the stress of competitive games triggered Travis. She studied her son's face. It was blank, void of excitement, interest, or nervousness.

"Checkers or chess?" Mason asked, pointing at a box of assorted plastic pieces.

As Travis lifted a black horse-head figure, Helen placed her hand over her mouth. *Chess! He should play checkers. He doesn't know anything about chess.*

After collecting the white figures, Mason placed them on the board. "I go first."

Travis mirrored the placement of his pieces, then leaned forward, his eyes fixed on the board. She was impressed by how quickly he had positioned the various shaped chessmen.

"Chess is fun, but hard," Mason said.

Miss Patterson, the librarian, walked around the room as game time began. She paused by the table and asked both boys, "Have you played chess before?"

Mason grinned. "Of course."

Travis shook his head without lifting his eyes from the board.

"Let me review the moves each piece can make," she said, showing how the various figures changed position and explained ranks and files.

Travis remained silent, his eyes never moving from the board.

Helen hoped her son could remember the different movements. As she watched, the two boys began their game.

Several moves later, Mason scratched his head. "Are you sure you haven't played before?"

Without hesitation, Travis moved his queen. The other boy frowned.

From where she sat, Helen observed the corners of Travis's mouth curl upward in a slight grin. She didn't understand the intricacies of chess, but the body language of both boys suggested that Travis was winning.

A few minutes later, Mason sighed. "You're supposed to say checkmate."

"Checkmate," Travis whispered.

Her eyes stung, and she fought back a tear that threatened to roll down her cheek. Travis hardly spoke to anyone, and here he was talking to a boy he didn't know.

Mason shrugged and knocked his king over. "Wow. You sure did that fast."

At the end of the session, Miss Patterson circulated through the room and spoke to Helen. "If your son is interested in chess, we have two members of the local chess club coming next week to demonstrate a more advanced version of chess. You are both invited to attend. The details are on a flyer by the door."

"Thanks," she said. "But my son never played chess before. He may not be ready for an advanced version. If he's interested, we'll be here."

Driving home, she glanced in the rearview mirror and saw Travis's hands moving as though he were shifting invisible game pieces in the air. *Is he replaying the game?* she wondered.

A week later, Helen and Travis entered the library game room. Two gray-haired men sat at a table with three glass chessboards stacked one above the other. Travis tugged on her arm. She looked down and saw his wide eyes. A grin lit up his face as he pointed to the tri-level boards. His excitement thrilled her.

Miss Patterson motioned for everyone to take a seat. "We're delighted to welcome two chess masters, Mr. Brad Lawson and Mr. Cliff Jergen, from the community chess club. They'll show us how tri-dimensional chess is played."

Brad Lawson stood up slowly. "Thank you for that kind introduction, but you can just call us Brad and Cliff," he said, then gestured toward the game board. "Chess is a game of strategy between two players. A chess board has sixty-four squares arranged in ranks and files. Each player has sixteen pieces. Today, we are going to show you a more advanced type of chess called 3-D chess. Cliff and I love playing this game."

The two men began the game and explained each of their moves. "All the pieces can move up or down levels, except the pawns," Cliff said.

Helen frowned. The squares all had names, and the players kept repeating the combination of letters and numbers for each square as they moved around the board. Keeping track of their moves was making her head hurt. But when she looked at Travis, his eyes were fixed on the three stacked boards. His body tilted forward.

After fifteen minutes, the two men nodded at each other, and Cliff rose. "We're going to stop playing and reset the board. We'd like to have someone volunteer to play Brad. I'll coach you, so don't worry about all the rules. Who would like to try 3-D chess?"

Before she could stop him, Travis jumped up and ran to the empty seat across from Brad. She blinked in surprise.

"Looks like we have our volunteer," Cliff said, standing beside Travis.

The audience clapped. Helen took a deep breath and prayed her son wouldn't have a meltdown. Studying Travis's smiling face, she felt a warm glow inside, crossed her fingers, and relaxed.

The chess pieces were set up, and although Cliff leaned close to Travis and pointed to where each piece went, Travis seemed to manage with limited guidance.

Move after move, pawns, bishops, rooks, and queens rapidly advanced across, up, and down the boards. The line of captured pieces next to Travis's side of the board grew.

She noticed Brad and Cliff exchanging glances. Their eyes shone with interest and awe. Her son's gaze never left the boards.

Suddenly, Travis said in a clear voice, "Have I ever mentioned you play a very irritating game of chess, Mr. Spock?"

With a chuckle, Brad replied, "Irritating? Ah yes, one of your Earth emotions." He winked at Travis.

Startled, Helen recognized the dialogue from her son's favorite *Star Trek* episode.

Travis and Cliff were still playing when the librarian stepped forward. "I'm afraid our time is up for today. I hope you liked this demonstration."

"We enjoyed being here," Brad said while Cliff nodded in agreement.

Helen went to Travis's side and thanked the chess masters. Her hand rested lightly on her son's shoulder.

"You should be proud of him," Brad said. "His spatial understanding is impressive for one so young."

Cliff gave Travis a high five. "You, young man, are a natural. We would love to have you join our chess club as a junior member."

Surprised at the offer, Helen swallowed hard, then gestured for Cliff to step aside with her.

"My son isn't . . ." She searched for the right word. "He isn't comfortable in certain situations."

"Our club is full of unique individuals. A love of chess unites us. He would fit right in. He has a gift for strategy, an innate understanding of how the pieces support each other, and a rather unshakeable focus. We're chess players; we thrive on challenges."

Helen glanced at Travis, who continued to play the game with Brad. She smiled and beamed with pride at the new direction Travis's life had just taken. "I believe he would like that," she said happily, adding, "and so would I."

Grand Opening

by Lona A. Smith

E ver since the concept of a hotel being built in outer space, I had been obsessed with the idea of being there for the grand opening.

"You're crazy," my mate said. "It's impossible."

"It's not," I answered and set out to prove it.

For the last three years as we traveled from our winter home in Mexico to our summer residence in upstate New York, I had been watching the progress at the NASA launch sites. This year on our journey north, I asked Mate to stay behind with me as I studied Starbase in Boca Chica, Texas where Starship manufacturing, testing, and launching occurred. In Texas, Mate complained that food in that area was hard to find and that it wasn't very good.

He had become annoyed with me when I wanted to divert from the usual route to fly over the Canaveral site in Florida and remain there in the fall, when the rest of our group continued south to yet warmer weather.

"What do you hope to accomplish?" he asked."

"I want to see how payloads are prepared and delivered," I replied.

"Payload," he sputtered. "Now you're even talking their lingo."

"I want to see how they load their merchandise, food, and human cargo. Besides, the food and sleeping accommodations are much better in Florida than they were in Texas." I cocked my head and smiled. He smiled back. So, we stayed behind.

The launch pads themselves are isolated and bleak because of the intensity of the heat and the space needed for blast off, so we had to travel a distance to the staging area to inspect it. We are known for our good eyesight, so I managed to fly among all that activity unnoticed. Sometimes Mate tagged along.

We argued, but I had an answer for every argument.

"It's too far," Mate said.

"It's not," I replied. "Satellites in Low Earth Orbit band are only from one hundred miles to twelve hundred miles above the Earth. We can travel that far in a day."

"But *that* is straight up," he said. "We won't be able to breathe."

"We'll be in the space ship, silly," I said. "We'll eat well before we're loaded and then we'll go into our torpor mode and hibernate for a few hours. When we wake up, we'll be there."

"And what happens when we get there?" Mate asked.

That pleased me because I could tell he was getting interested.

"The ship lands on the docking hub in the middle of the satellite. There's a lot of activity there because it is also the operation and control center," I explained. "It's like a spinning wheel with spoke-like shafts that are the elevators. Guests and employees travel through these to get to the main lobby and to the guest rooms. The rooms are in the part of the wheel that encircles the structure the way a tire does a wheel. It's the spinning that creates the artificial gravity. We won't fall off," I assured him.

"We need a lot of food to survive. What will we eat?" Mate asked.

I rolled my eyes. Just like a man, thinking about his stomach. "I'll figure that out," I said.

"How long will we stay?" Mate asked.

"I'm four years old," I said quietly. "I won't be coming back,"

Mate disappeared for a few days. Unlike others in our avian species, we do not mate for life.

My excitement grew when March 10, 2027 was announced as the date for the hotel's grand opening. A week's stay was to cost nearly a million dollars. That year we again stayed behind in Canaveral. I have to admit that it made me sad to say farewell to our family and traveling companions. Mate was nowhere to be found; he's not good at goodbyes.

We took up residence in a nearby property filled with luscious plants and trees. I watched as payloads of furniture, supplies, and employees were sent up in ships that left the pad in January and February. Then, about a week before the opening date, I saw trucks roll in to the staging area loaded with small trees and large plants in the back. The plants were in full foliage and bloom. They were beautiful.

"We have to go," I told Mate.

"Why?"

"Because this is how we're going to get on board," I said. "This is our chance. This is what I've been waiting for. We have to go now. I'm flying." I flew but wasn't sure he would follow.

I targeted a beautiful hibiscus plant filled with rose colored blossoms and dove directly into it. My heart was so full I didn't think it could beat any faster, but it did when I felt Mate land beside me. We made our way to the center branches and dug our toes that are made especially for hanging on into the green fiber.

We were bounced around as burlap was tightly secured around the plants and when we were loaded into the ship's cargo area. But we were used to being bounced around in stormy weather, so we hung on. We were then slid into some kind of hollow cylinder and were able to get a little nourishment from a blossom near us. Then we went into our torpor state and dozed until we heard voices. The humans had arrived. We couldn't see anything but identified the crew and some other voices that sounded *very* important.

"When do we leave?" Mate whispered.

I heard a rumble as the booster rockets ignited. "Soon," I said. "Very soon."

I hadn't told him the part about liftoff because I'm sure he wouldn't have come. I hadn't told him that the first couple of minutes would be very uncomfortable; that this part of the flight is hugely physical, with g-forces three times normal. I imagined it might be like flying into a tornado or hurricane. There is also a high-frequency vibration that is painful as the ship pushes its way through the thick air of Earth. By that time we're high enough so that, as the air thins and the boosters explode off in a burst of flames, we're comfortable.

We waited. We dozed and, without warning, it happened. We were flung against the burlap that was plastered against the wall of the container. The noise *was* excruciating. We felt ourselves becoming lighter. We weren't holding on; we weren't flying; we were floating. It might have been an hour. It might have been two. I had no way of telling.

We felt some thuds when we landed. I thought someone had squashed me. I picked myself up and looked for Mate. He was lying at my feet. His usually vibrant plumage was pale and disheveled. We had barely enough energy to hang on when we were moved again and the cylinder was opened. We were placed in those tube-like elevators I'd read about and had a more gentle ride that lasted a few minutes. Poking through a hole in the burlap, I could see that we were now in the lobby. After being shifted this way and that, we were finally secured into what was to be *our place*. The burlap was removed, and I looked out on a beautifully appointed area.

"Wow!" I heard Mate whisper beside me. I turned, and I think my heart stopped for a moment. Tears sprang into my eyes at the magnificence of the scene before me. We were gliding smoothly among the stars. Although we had seen Earth from the sky, it had never been like this. When activity died down, we found that with artificial gravity we were able to fly anywhere we wanted. By using our sharp beaks to puncture a drink pouch carried by employees, we soon discovered a new nectar called *sweet tea*. Then we would fly from room to room taking in indescribable views.

By the time the first guests arrived the following week, I was already building my nest, because no distance is too far, and no dimension is too great or too small for a hummingbird who wants to be present for the grand opening of the Hotel in the Sky.

Grandma's Wisdom

by Bobbie Thiessen

Cigarette smoke and the smell of stale beer greeted Brandy as she entered the dive bar. The sound system blared classic rock—Tom Petty's "Running Down a Dream"—and glasses clinked as the bartenders poured drinks.

Brandy found it hard to breathe and fought back the bile that filled her throat as she spotted Grayson, the man who told her just the night before that he loved her. He sat at the end of the bar with a hand on Denise's thigh.

Why did he lie to me? What did he gain? Why tell me he loved me if he didn't?

Brandy had heard the rumors about Grayson and Denise, the woman he insisted was "just a friend." She suspected Grayson hadn't been truthful when he claimed to be working late or hanging with the boys.

Brandy watched in silence as Denise caressed Grayson's shoulder, and he leaned in to kiss her.

She's pretty but not any prettier than me. She drinks as much as Grayson. Maybe that's the attraction.

Brandy gave the couple one last look before exiting the bar.

As she maneuvered her Chevrolet Malibu out of the small parking lot, Brandy reflected on the red flags she had failed to notice—or maybe chose to ignore. Like the times they would make plans to attend an event only to have Grayson cancel at the last minute, or the time he claimed to have been so ill, he decided to stay in his apartment in the northern part of the state rather than return to his home in Orlando. His boss rented the apartment, so Grayson didn't have to move from hotel to hotel when his work kept him near the Florida-Georgia line. Less than a week after Grayson's "illness," Brandy saw pictures Grayson's friend Lily posted on her Facebook page of her long weekend stay at Grayson's apartment.

He never even invited me to his house here in Orlando. What kind of fool have I been?

The worse time for me was when Grayson claimed he wouldn't date me because he was still mourning his late fiancée.

"It's not just you," he said. "I don't date anyone. I just can't right now."

Two nights after the no-date talk, Brandy was with friends at another bar when Grayson walked in with Lily.

Why was I such a fool?

The tears Brandy had been holding back streamed down her face as she parked her car in her driveway. She struggled with the lock, finally getting the front door open as sobs shook her body.

"Was he a person you really wanted to be in a relationship with?" Brandy could hear her deceased grandmother's voice and caught a whiff of Tabu, the perfume her grandmother always wore. The rocking chair Brandy inherited after her grandmother's death creaked and moved slightly. Before cancer took her grandmother's life, she provided emotional support as Brandy survived divorce, cheating boyfriends, and loss of jobs. Her grandmother was the one person who encouraged Brandy to follow her dreams and who never criticized or judged her.

I think I always knew Grayson was leading me on, Brandy admitted. *The funny thing is I wasn't looking for a boyfriend when we started talking. I just wanted a friend. Then I got sick and had to have surgery. During my recovery, Grayson told me he loved me. Why did he do that? Why did he have to come into my life?*

Was I never good enough? I knew no one would love me or find me attractive after the doctors cut my chest open. Why did Grayson give me hope?

"Oh, rubbish."

Her grandmother's voice was so strong and so loud that it was as if she was sitting in Brandy's living room and not just living in her head. "You aren't the first woman to survive open heart surgery, and your physical scars are hardly noticeable. You're going to let a man decide if you have value? Girl, didn't I teach you anything?

"Remember, everything happens for a reason," grandmother's voice continued.

"I want to believe that Grandma, but I don't understand why I always end up alone. Why can't girls like Denise and Lily have struggles?"

"They probably do, just not the same ones as you. No one escapes this world without encountering a little pain. I know it feels like you've had more than your share of pain and heartbreak.

"I think part of your problem is you continue to pick the wrong type of man to get involved with. Think of the things you don't like about Grayson. Be honest now. We know no man is perfect."

"No, he definitely isn't perfect." Brandy smiled. "Most days, he drinks a case of beer and at least a half bottle of Jameson's. He's self-centered. He's lied to me several times."

"What happened to your two strikes rule?"

"I know," Brandy said. "I should have banned him from my life after the second lie. For some reason . . ."

"Oh, girl, don't give me that bull."

"Grandma!"

"And don't 'Grandma' me. You know I'm right. You're not the only one who's had problems with the opposite sex. Your grandfather—loved that man—he was just as self-centered as your father. Maybe that's why you keep picking self-centered men. On some level they remind you of the first man you loved—your father.

"After your grandfather died, I made a point of insisting that the men in my life treat me with respect."

"Is that why you never remarried?" Brandy asked.

"In my day, few men wanted to raise another man's children. When your grandfather died, I had a half dozen children still living at home. The youngest was just three. Your grandfather and I survived the Depression and years of drought and bad crops. We lost our general store and the first farm we owned."

"I know you had it rough, Grandma."

"Everyone has rough times. I'm not looking for pity. I'm just reminding you that rough times and people who hurt us are just part of life. Every person who comes into your life adds something. Maybe it's just to teach you a lesson. So, what's the lesson you learned from Grayson?"

"Not to trust men."

"Seriously?"

"Okay, maybe to trust my instincts?"

"You asking or telling?" her grandmother asked.

"Telling. In the future, I need to trust my instincts and refuse to settle. I won't make excuses for any man—or for myself. It's okay to sometimes put myself first."

"So, fix your makeup and go grab a cup of coffee," her grandmother said.

"I miss you, Grandma," Brandy whispered as her grandmother's voice faded and the rocking chair stopped moving.

———

Two hours later, Brandy walked into the Cuban coffee shop in downtown Winter Park. As she paid for her twelve-ounce café con leche, she bumped into the tall gray-haired man standing behind her.

"Excuse me," she said.

"No, excuse me." The man smiled, and his seafoam-green eyes looked directly into hers.

"My fault." Brandy smiled back. "Sometimes I can't get out of my own way."

POETRY

Upon the Loss of an Old Friend

by Angela Adee Andriesse

Dear Joe Cohen, saxophonist:
I knew you and you knew me.
When we were away from home for the first time
At "College." A new dimension.

I knew I was misplaced—almost immediately.
But you—
You were part genius,   part—what?
Evel Knievel doing stunts in Jazz Forum at 1 o'clock on Fridays.

My jazz was words.
But yours—
You were this young kid that would just shred—
Or so they said—I still don't know what that means—
Nor do I care—But I do know you had something inside you.
Something to say: Different. Special. Scattered. Clamoring. Urgent.
Searching.

An overdose, they said.
Spent time living on the streets, they said.
You had asked for money, they said.
Were the streets of San Francisco cruel or kind?   I'm thinking cruel.

One night—I doubt either one of us was 20 yet—
At a party, I pulled you out to the cars
And in secret I asked you to score me some coke.
(God—have I rendered myself utterly ridiculous?)
I wanted to be emaciated, you see,
And I thought coke could help me get there.
I wanted to be emaciated—to eventually disappear.
To no longer need anything/anyone/anymore.

You say NO to me.

You said NO—saw yourself in me.
If only someone had extended that same kindness
To you
Before the first time.   Before the end began.

I can still listen to you online.
Of course—it's not the same as when I would hear you in the distance
Through my dorm window—playing soprano sax in the music school
courtyard.
Something new you were trying out.
Nothing is the same as that.

When we were 19 and your aunt had just passed away
You said: "She knows everything now."
Now you get to know all the unknowable shit
You can stop searching for all the mysteries—
You know them.

You knew me once and I knew you.
Now you know everything.

Love always, and I f–ing mean *always*,

Your friend—Golden Lady

A Measure of Love

by Ann Favreau

I don't need a ruler to measure my love for him.
Inches quickly disappear as I kiss him goodnight.
Loving gazes slide yards across the room.
My arms encircle him gauging our affection.

Miles evaporate when I leave him at day care
knowing my love clings like a crazy quilt
without a millimeter of empty space,
secure until I return to his broad smile.

I won't use a ruler to measure my love for him
but draw a straight line ———— from my heart to his.

Maroon Moccasins

by Gail Ghai

And I will dress in purple velvet pants
with a purple silk blouse,
soft and succulent as grapes.

I'll carry an oversized fuchsia evening bag
etched with threads of foxglove glitz and greed
that'll match my plumbago stockings.

I'll show up at mass in maroon moccasins,
a burgundy headdress, and a beaded lavender dress
with fringes that shake like lilacs.
I shall learn, finally, to Raindance.

I can't wait to turn old, when, like juveniles
I can live on the *I don't give a damn* edge—
as I stuff myself into a tutu of amethyst,
too close to my folding skins.
And the magenta tongues of critics will flutter
like the wings of a Purple emperor.

Then I'll strut into the supermarket,
two violet parrots strapped to each shoulder.
I'll rattle the orderly carts,

whistle long lyrical wolf whistles.
And when the sweaty polite manager tells me:
NO PARROTS ALLOWED—
I'll say: *What parrots? They're shoulder pads.*

But for now, I'll coast in grays.
Stroll through my ashen life,
that slow silver path to a senior bus pass.
But keep in mind, I'm a February child.
Purple is only a hue away.

Fledging

by Sylvia Whitman

Fledging applies to both parent and chick.
We both know it's time for you to leave the nest.
You are my first, but the second left you behind.
That's been the gall of your childhood.

We both know it's time for you to leave the nest.
We're chafing as roommates, lark and night owl.
That's been the gall of your childhood.
We're so very different.

We're chafing as roommates, lark and night owl.
We're not cut out for matching mother-daughter outfits.
We're so very different.
I think you smarter, more capable, than you give me credit for.

We're not cut out for matching mother-daughter outfits.
You think I'm too idealistic, all rainbow and unicorns.
I think you smarter, more capable, than you give me credit for.
You want to prove you don't need me.

You think I'm too idealistic, all rainbow and unicorns.
I worry that you worry too much.
You want to prove you don't need me.
I want that too, up to a point.

I worry that you worry too much.
You tell me I should get out more.
I want that too, up to a point.
We are a push-me-pull-you.

You tell me I should get out more.
"Don't you dare cry," you shoot across my bow.
We are a push-me-pull-you.
It's time for both of us, each of us, to spread our wings.

"Don't you dare cry," you shoot across my bow,
  as I co-sign your lease as guarantor.
It's time for both of us, each of us, to spread our wings.
Fledging applies to both parent and chick.

The Atoms Align at Last

by Kathleen Willoughby

I've done to you what women do:
led you to believe, not
that you were needed —
but that I would end—without you.

In truth, I can mend a broken bone,
soothe a birthing mother's cry with song,
fix a flat tire, satisfy my desire,
and cook my favorite meal for one.

I prefer to dance alone.
Yet, I made myself small to fit.
Then smaller still. A tiny star inside
the static universe of you.

Now, I am commanding as a pulsing
planet; demanding as a black hole.

I am stardust once more,
belonging to no one.

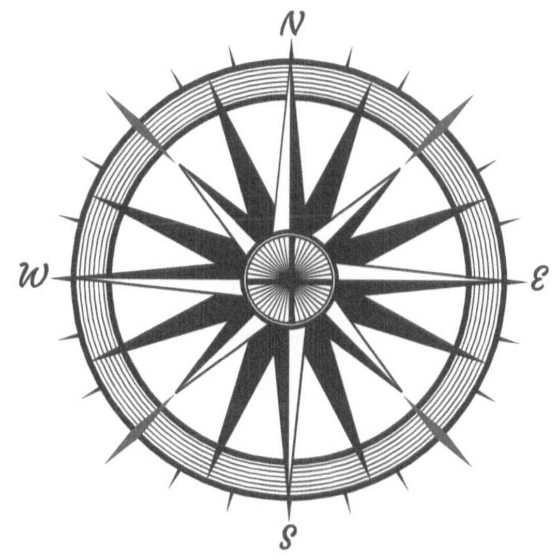

NEXTGEN POETRY

The New Way

by Finn Anderson

When you think of a direction
You think of an
Arrow pointing
To a land far far away
But it's really a place

You pick to go every day
There are millions of
Directions like little anthills
With little ant people
Filling in

Where the ants wave me to come
You can choose but
The best direction is
The one no man has ever
Gone

Dreams

by Perla Anderson

It washes over me
Holds me in its safe cocoon
Can be peace or peril
Sorrow or serene
Captivates me in its endless depths or shallow pools
Swirling my thoughts like Van Gogh
Taking scraps of past and present
Knitting together a cloak of black
Drowning, falling, pain
Dancing, fairies, paintings
You never know what you will see
When drifting off into the world of dreams

Shifting Horizons

by Reed Barnwell

We step into the silent dawn,
A world where shadows stretch and yawn,
The air hums with whispered plans,
As time slips through our open hands.

A river winds like silver threads,
Flowing through the dreams we've shed,
Its current soft, but strong and clear,
Pulls us toward the unknown frontier.

The stars above with glowing eyes,
Watch our journey as it flies,
And winds that weave through tangled trees
Speak in voices on the breeze.

Each step we take, a door ajar,
Leading us to lands afar,
In these new dimensions, we will find,
The endless paths that free the mind.

The Synthetic Frontier

by Genevieve Blitch

This Synthetic Frontier is uncharted and new
An art just waiting to be grasped
It must be explored through and through

It's a freshly coded path just within view
It sits at my fingertips mysterious and masked
This Synthetic Frontier is uncharted and new

I began to question if its responses would be true?
As I wait for the answers to be thoroughly unpacked
It must be explored through and through

Is this Synthetic Frontier necessary to subdue?
This AI's responses are beyond contrast
This Synthetic Frontier is uncharted and new

I continue, to read and suspiciously review
The answer I'd thought for myself has been greatly surpassed
This Synthetic Frontier is uncharted and new
It must be explored through and through

Fish●ing

by Conner Brown

To some just line, to some just time
To me a peace, like a release.

My mind gets clear, happiness draws near
No speaking phone, just me alone.

My heart is full, nothing's in control
My thoughts run free; I can just be.

I grab my bait, no more wait
My cast the sound, splash, nobody around.

My reasons are mostly mine; I'll tell in time.
Space I need, this day; it feeds.

I can raise my voice, noise, my choice
I learned this new place helps me grow
It makes me whole, this I know.

Worlds Beyond, Yet Within

by Wilson Tyler

There are many worlds out there
I'm not quite sure where.
Maybe more than worlds
Maybe universes, stretching arms wide,
Waiting to be discovered.
But there's one thing I know
Everything has to grow.
Maybe we should explore this wild,
Like a curious child.
And if we change our perspective,
We can receive a new directive.
Change our ways to preserve, not destroy
Explore the new, yet cherish what we have.
It could be a barren desert I see
Or maybe a lush forest
But no matter what we must not
Stop seeking the new.

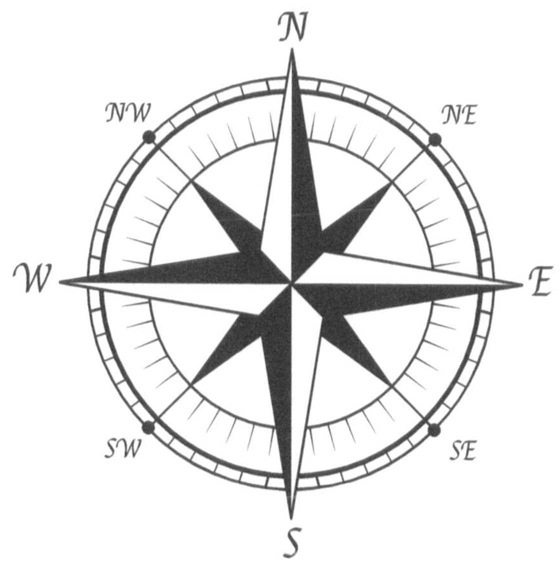

CONTRIBUTOR BIOS

Adult Members

Gerri Almand- Gerri found her writing voice when she was sweet-talked into buying an RV after retiring. Three award-winning humorous RV travel books later, Gerri now rails against growing old as she struggles to adjust to life in an over-55 community in the quirky Pacific Northwest.

Angela Adee Andriesse - Angela is a PhD student at Florida Atlantic University, a high school English teacher, and an adjunct professor. Her work explores neurodivergence, life writing, and identity. She writes to honor overlooked stories and to imagine more inclusive ways of learning, knowing, and being.

Lynn Bechdolt- Lynn is a retired Lutheran pastor who shares her home with a red dog and writes whatever comes to mind.

Barbara A. Busenbark- Barbara is a writer, painter, and eternal optimist; her creative energies drive her free-spirited approach to life. Her memoir, *Uncharted,* is the embodiment of her sense of adventure and determination. Published in 2024, it takes the reader down the Intracoastal Waterway in search of healing. Barbara served as this year's Collection's cover designer.

Deborah Crutcher- Deb, a retired speech pathologist, writes creative nonfiction and poetry. She is a member of the Key West Poetry Society and the Winter Haven Writers group. She currently resides in Central Florida. Her work has been published in various media, including a collection of poetry and a memoir/self-help book.

Scott Corey- Scott is the award-winning author of *Whistling for Hippos* and *Elephants in Paris.* He spends his time in St. Augustine, Kansas City, and Europe.

L.H. Davis (Laurance Howard Davis III)- Laurance holds a degree in mechanical engineering and lives in Melbourne, Florida. He has self-published over ten novels. Laurance won *L. Ron Hubbard's Writers of the Future* contest in 2022 and the RPLAs in 2011, 2013, and 2024.

Nanette Davis- Nanette is an author and retired professional educator. She has won awards for her short stories and published a memoir in 2019 entitled *Orphan Tales: A Search for Truth, Love and Family*. She completed her first novel in 2023. She resides in St. Petersburg, Florida.

Margaret Daisley- Margaret (Peg) is a freelance editor living in St. Petersburg, Florida. She especially loves working on memoirs and is finally getting back to doing some writing herself. She has published nonfiction stories and essays in parenting and women's magazines and in academic journals.

Diana Faherty- After more than 40 years as an editor, Diana Faherty is rediscovering the joy of writing. She lives and plays in Ormond Beach in a 100-year-old house.

Christina Farinas- Cristina is a poet and fiction writer whose work often explores themes of environmental and wildlife conservation as well as the journey of self-discovery. Her poetry has been published both in Florida and as far away as New Zealand. When she's not writing, Cristina enjoys photography and hiking.

Ann Favreau- Ann, a retired educator, is president of the Suncoast Writers Guild. She has self-published six books. Her latest *The Dementia Spiral* was an RPLA semifinalist. Ann loves sharing her work and gives presentations to local women's and civic groups.

James R. Garrison- Jim has written and self-published three novels. He is a member of the Manatee Writers Group in Bradenton, Florida. Jim favors novels, short stories, and poetry. His story "Becoming" was published in FWA's Collection 16, *Metamorphosis*.

Lorrie Gault- Lorrie is a transplanted Virginian now living in Central Florida with her husband and rescue cats. She finds bears, manatees, and rocket launches endlessly fascinating. Someday soon they no doubt will appear in her stories. This is her second publication in FWA's Collection.

Gail Ghai- Gail is a poet, teacher, workshop leader, Pushcart Prize nominee, and author of four chapbooks including her upcoming poetry collection, *Aerodynamics* from Finishing Line Press. Her poetry has appeared in *Poet Lore, The Malahat Review, JAMA,* and *Shot Glass Journal.* She is moderator of the Ringling Poets in Sarasota, Florida.

David Godin- Dave is retired from corporate life and the US Air Force; now he spends his days writing his memoir, golfing, volunteering, walking his dog, Jake, and driving his wife Lisa to distraction. *Five Minutes* published Dave's essay titled "Daily Ritual." Jake says Dave has been impossible to live with ever since.

Bill Griffith- Bill won the 2023 RPLA in the Young Adult/New Adult category. He's a member of Florida Writers Association, the Manatee Writers Group, the International Thriller Writers, and the Society of Children's Book Writers and Illustrators. He has also served as an RPLA judge.

Ellen P. Holder- Ellen has just published a mystery novel but also writes romance, poetry, and flash fiction, and she freelances as a copyeditor. She has been published in previous FWA Collections. For the past fifteen years, Ellen has performed with her husband at dance parties all across Central Florida.

John Hope- John is an award-winning short-story, middle-grade, young-adult, science-fiction, fantasy, and historical fiction writer with over 20 published novels. His writing has been included in over 50 story collections. He travels the country providing inspirational and informative presentations to schools and writing groups. His best friends are pink panthers.

Sharon Keller Johnson- Although born in Allentown, Pennsylvania, Sharon Keller Johnson has lived in Florida since 1981 and considers herself a Pennsylvania Dutch-Italian-Floridian. She enjoys Lebanese bologna, cooks schnitzel, uses y'all, and eats grits. When not writing, Sharon paints, teaches, and has adventures with her dog, Molly the Maltipoo.

Henry Jame Kaye- Born and raised in Pittsburgh, Henry's writing has earned the RPLA in Unpublished Book of the Year. He has won multiple RPLAs and been included in numerous volumes of FWA's Collections. His work also has appeared in the *Deadliest Games* anthology, the *2023 Farmer's Almanac*, and many news outlets. He lives with his wife, Nancy, in New Smyrna Beach, Florida.

Brenda K. Lavieri- Brenda writes with heart and purpose, drawing on personal experiences to explore themes of connectedness. She lives in Tennessee with husband Ed and their polydactyl cat Bougie. She runs a tableware brand, loves good coffee, and cherishes frequent trips to Amelia Island.

KE Manning- KE is a Florida-based author whose work spans dystopia, magical realism, and literary fiction. She writes about people on the edge of systems, of survival, of becoming. When not writing, she grows food, raises kids, and plots chaos in the sunshine.

Chris Marek- Chris writes short fiction and autobiographical nonfiction stories and has enjoyed seeing his work recognized by the FWA. He lives in Gulfport, Florida and likes to recharge his creative energy by gardening, exercising, and hiking.

Meredith S. Martin- Meredith a is a retired lawyer. She spends her winters in Summerfield, Florida and summers in Jasper, Georgia with her dog Mandy and cat Cali. When not reading, she photographs sunsets, dabbles in painting, and takes leisurely walks with Mandy.

Robert E. Marvin- Robert is a member of Florida Writers, FWA Manatee Chapter, and heads The Renaissance Authors critiquing group. Several of his short stories have appeared in the FWA's Collections and *The Florida Writer* magazine.

Mark H. Newhouse- Mark was an FWA Director, Youth Chairperson, and multi-year RPLA medalist. *The Devil's Bookkeepers*, suspenseful novels set in the Holocaust, was honored as RPLA's Published Book of the Year and Chanticleer International Book Awards' Grand Prize Fiction Series. "The Defenders of Monstrovia" are mystery podcasts free on Amazon.

Donna Parrey- Donna writes essays, poetry, children's books, nonfiction, short fiction and continues to explore new writing horizons and hone her craft. A writer will forever be a work in progress. She is based in St. Petersburg, Florida.

William R. Platt- William writes speculative fiction in the realms of sci-fi, fantasy, and horror genres. His short stories have appeared in the FWA's Collections 14, 15, 16, and 17. He also served as president of the Suncoast Writers Guild and as an RPLA judge.

Barbara Ryan- Barbara, emerita professor of sociology, has published books and articles on feminism, the women's movement, and identity politics. She is a past president of Florida Gulf Coast Sister in Crime. Her story "Are You Afraid of Monsters?" was included in *Paradise is Deadly*, an anthology she co-edited. She also writes murder mysteries.

H.G. Silvia- H.G.'s passion for spinning mind-bending yet satisfying yarns that entertain and evoke thoughts long after reading them are goals he strives to meet in all his works. He is an active member of the Brandon Writers Critique Group and the Tarpon Springs Fiction Writers Group.

K.L. Small- K. L. writes novels and stories for the young and young at heart. She lives on a horse ranch in Brooksville with her husband, two horses, four barn cats, and assorted wildlife. Her latest book is *Letters from Shadow Oaks*, a women's fiction.

Lona A. Smith- Lona has been a member of FWA since 2005. She is the author of two published novels and one biography, two of which were RPLA winners. She also has had several of her short stories published in Collection volumes. Recently she has become a Florida resident.

Bobbie Thiessen- Bobbie, a retired technical writer and instructional systems designer, lives in Winter Park. When not writing, she enjoys reading, listening to live music, and attending outdoor festivals.

Stan Watkins- Stan is a former Hoosier and Connecticut Yankee. He now lives in St. Augustine, Florida. He has owned and operated a successful mystery dinner theater—Crime & Merriment Mysteries, LLC—since 1995. Stan has completed a novel titled *Dudleytown* and was previously published in a recipe book for the Danbury Library.

Sylvia Whitman- Sylvia teaches writing at Ringling College in Sarasota. She's published hundreds of articles for adults and more than a dozen books for young readers, including novels *The Milk of Birds* (Atheneum 2013, YA) and *Decide & Survive: The Destruction of Pompeii* (Bushel & Peck 2024, MG).

Kathleen Willoughby- Kathleen is a retired marketing executive, currently residing in Central Florida. She writes poetry, short stories, and essays. Her poetry has been performed at various venues, including The Bowery Poetry Club, Bluestockings Bookstore, and the Fresh Fruit Festival. Her poems and essays have been published in anthologies and newspapers.

NextGen Members

Finn Anderson- Finn is twelve years old and goes to Spark Middle School in Naples Florida. In his free time, he likes to play with his dog, Winne, and his rabbit, Yoka. He also enjoys playing tennis and pickleball. His favorite cuisine is Italian and he never tires of eating homemade sourdough bread

Perla Anderson- Perla is an 8th grader attending a middle school in Naples, Florida. In her free time, she enjoys hanging out with friends, going to the beach, and attending youth groups.

Reed Barnwell- Reed is a student at Spark Hybrid Education Center. He plays tennis and flag football. His favorite subjects are math and science.

Genevieve Blitch- Genevieve is thirteen years old; she likes to play tennis and is planning on getting her Eagle Scout rank within the next two years.

Conner Brown- Conner is a kind, and curious person. His favorite subjects are science and history, and he inspires to become a doctor. This year he made his acting debut. His favorite hobby is 3-D printing. He loves his dog, Indigo and spending time with his brother and sisters.

Wilson Tyler- Wilson goes to Spark of Southwest Florida, and enjoys reading in his free time. He wants to become a nuclear physicist when he grows up.

Editorial Staff

Rick Bettencourt- Rick is the author of multiple novels with over 90,000 copies sold. He crafts heartfelt fiction blending fantasy, showbiz, diverse LGBTQ+ characters, and humor. A Massachusetts native now living in Florida with his husband and dog, Rick passionately supports fellow writers and artists through Freedom Oak Media and leadership roles with the Florida Writers Association, empowering creatives to build meaningful, sustainable artistic journeys

Linda C. Wright- Before becoming a full-time writer, Linda worked as a C.P.A. Her memoir, *A Bittersweet Goodnight*, was the bronze winner for unpublished works in the 2019 RPLA. Her first fiction novel is titled *Hello Jaynie!* Linda's new release is *A Vacation with Strangers.* She now resides in Melbourne, Florida.

Michael Farrell- Michael was captivated by stories of all different forms as a child. Now he aspires to master the connection between writer and reader. He is Chairperson of the Florida Writers Association's Youth program, and has been featured in multiple FWA Collections.

Patricia Grayson- Patricia has been writing for several decades and uses her experience abroad in some of her work. She grew up overseas and is interested in history, poetry, and police procedural novels. Her many different jobs—pet shop owner, house painter, secretary, housecleaner—have made her life fascinating and have helped her raise two children with her husband of 43 years.

Michele Verbitski Knudsen- Michele recently completed a romantic mystery where fortune tellers, disguises, and crazy relatives, draw you into a tangled web of . . . murder. Over the years, she has judged for the

RPLA and Collection 17. Michele's short stories have appeared in four of FWA's Collection books and *The Florida Writer* magazine.

Linda Kraus- Linda is a professor of literature and cinema studies who has taught at colleges in the University of Massachusetts system and Case Western Reserve University. She's published two prize-winning collections: *Popcorn Icons and Other Poems Celebrating Movies* and *Listening to the Silence* available on Amazon and from Meat for Tea Press. Her poems have appeared in journals and poetry anthologies. She is completing a third collection expected to be published in 2026.

David M. Pearce- When he isn't writing, David works as a deputy attorney for Sarasota County. He holds a law degree from UF and a master of studies in environmental law from Vermont Law School. He ran a critique group in Bradenton, Florida for four years. His work has appeared in *The Florida Writer* magazine, FWA's annual Collections, *Animal Literary Magazine*, and on Medium. His sci-fi series has won several RPLAs. His favorite novels are those that transport him to fantasy and science fiction worlds.

ACKNOWLEDGEMENTS

I find it difficult to decide where to begin my thanks to the many individuals who made this year's collection of prose and poetry possible. But let me start with the most important people that breathed life into this book—our members who took the brave step of submitting their work. It is with heartfelt sincerity that I thank Florida Writers Association's members who allowed our editorial staff of Rick Bettencourt, Linda Courtwright, Patricia Grayson, Michael Farrell, Michele Knudsen, Linda Kraus, and David Pearce, to read their words.

As you hold this copy of *New Directions/New Dimensions* in your hands, take some time to appreciate the cover that wraps the stories and poems contained herein with an original photograph by our cover designer Barbara Busenbark. Her artistic eye is evident in the road's perspective, the water's reflections, and the background's undulating hills—all elements that evoke this year's Collection theme. It took months of patient collaboration to accomplish a cover that not only is a work of art but also tells a story.

And I would be remiss if I didn't express my appreciation to FWA president Mary Ann de Stefano who, over the past three years, has encouraged me to take bold new steps to bring Florida Writers Association's only print publication to a higher level. It is to Mary Ann and the entire FWA board that I extend my gratitude for your trust and continued support.

This year, Florida Writers Association is happy to have worked again with Arielle Haughee, owner of Orange Blossom Publishing. Thank you for your formatting services and assistance in bringing this book to print.

Paul Iasevoli, Collection 17,
Executive Editor